Pub Strolls in

CAMBRIDGESHIRE

Ady Collier

COUNTRYSIDE BOOKS
NEWBURY BERKSHIRE

First published 2002
© Ady Collier 2002

COUNTRYSIDE BOOKS
3 Catherine Road
Newbury, Berkshire

To view our complete range of books,
please visit us at
www.countrysidebooks.co.uk

ISBN 1 85306 736 9

Produced through MRM Associates Ltd., Reading
Printed in Italy

Contents

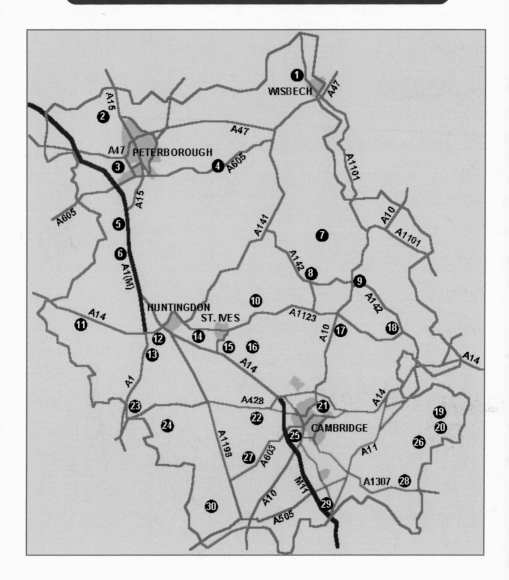

PUBLISHER'S NOTE

We hope that you obtain considerable enjoyment from this book; great care has been taken in its preparation. Although at the time of publication all routes followed public rights of way or permitted paths, diversion orders can be made and permissions withdrawn.

We cannot, of course, be held responsible for such diversion orders and any inaccuracies in the text which result from these or any other changes to the routes nor any damage which might result from walkers trespassing on private property. We are anxious though that all details covering the walks are kept up to date and would therefore welcome information from readers which would be relevant to future editions.

The simple sketch maps that accompany the walks in this book are based on notes made by the author whilst checking out the routes on the ground.

However, for the benefit of a proper map, we do recommend that you purchase the relevant Ordnance Survey sheet covering your walk. The Ordnance Survey maps are widely available, especially through booksellers and local newsagents.

Did you know that most of Cambridgeshire is even flatter than Norfolk? The highest point is only 480 feet and so it is ideal for some leisurely walking. Rich and fertile, the county has a largely rural countenance. The hills, mainly in the south and west of the county, form pleasant undulations on rolling green pastures and there are beautiful meadows that provide a home to a whole variety of wildlife. The meadows follow the meandering courses of the main regional rivers: the Cam, the Great Ouse and the Nene, and the walks in this book provide plenty of opportunity to indulge the spirit in their lazy flow. The Fens themselves were drained roughly 300 years ago, and nowadays form a vital habitat for numerous wading and waterbirds and many rare plant species.

Throughout Cambridgeshire there are many small wooded areas, often spookily atmospheric and some quite ancient. In addition, there are nearby man-made attractions to be visited. The world famous university city of Cambridge is beautiful, vibrant and unmissable, but it is merely one stop in a fascinating region. The county boasts many famous sons and daughters from the pages of history. Everyone recalls the poet Rupert Brooke, the man who put Grantchester on the literary map with his famous line about the local church clock indicating tea-time: 'and is there honey still for tea?' Oliver Cromwell represented Huntingdon in Parliament, as, more recently, did former Prime Minister John Major. A list of the famous people that have lived in Cambridgeshire over the years could probably fill this book alone.

Oh, and just for good measure, Robin Hood was known as the Earl of Huntingdon!

So far, I have said nothing about one of the greatest riches to be found in the county. I refer, of course, to the pubs. Often historic, never dull, the pubs in this book have been chosen for their friendly welcome, cheerful atmosphere, delicious food, and good beer (real ale). Some are set in isolated farmland, others by the riverside. Most have an unusual feature or two, and all have been enjoyable to visit and research for this book. Parking for patrons is available at the pubs whilst you do the walks but it is only courteous to seek permission before setting off.

The walks invariably follow public rights of way, only very occasionally venturing through areas of private land, and only then where permission to access a route is clearly signposted. The going underfoot can vary considerably with the seasons, so it's best to wear sturdy footwear. The maps included in the book are based on notes taken whilst researching the routes but please bear in mind that they are no more than sketches and in no way intended to replicate scaled mapping. It is always wise to have access to OS mapping, and reference to the relevant OS Explorer series map is included for each walk.

I hope you have as much fun on these walks as I have. Finally, do remember to follow the Country Code, avoid leaving litter and check that all gates are carefully shut behind you. Happy strolling!

Ady Collier

Leverington
The Rising Sun

MAP: OS EXPLORER 235 (GR 445108)   **WALK 1**   **DISTANCE:** 3½ MILES

DIRECTIONS TO START: FOLLOW THE A47, A17 OR A141/A47 TO THE A1101. THEN FOLLOW THE A1101 TO THE JUNCTION WITH THE B1169. FOLLOW THE B1169 TO THE JUNCTION SIGNPOSTED TO LEVERINGTON. THE RISING SUN IS SITUATED AT THIS JUNCTION. **PARKING:** IN THE PUB CAR PARK.

The thriving village of Leverington is situated to the far north of Cambridgeshire, just to the north-west of the scenic fenland market town of Wisbech. This is fruit growing country and orchards are therefore in plentiful supply. St Leonard's church in the centre of the village is well worth a visit. Built of Barnack stone in the Early English and Perpendicular styles, its tall steeple is surrounded by four small turrets.

The walk, for the main part, follows quiet village roads and well defined pathways and there are excellent views over the rich fertile farmland surrounding the village.

The Rising Sun

This comfortable two-bar pub dates from the 17th century. There is a log fire for those colder winter days, and a warm welcome all year round. It is open Monday to Saturday from 11.30 am to 2 pm and from 7 pm to 11 pm. On Sunday, it is open from 12 noon to 2 pm and from 7 pm to 11 pm.

Beers are Elgood's Cambridge Bitter, Greyhound Strong Bitter and Black Dog Mild. A good selection of wines and bottled ales is also offered. There is a wide and sumptuous food menu available, every day of the week, 12 noon to 2 pm and 7 pm to 10 pm. Telephone: 01945 583754.

The Walk

① From the Rising Sun turn right and follow the road to St Leonard's church, signposted to Leverington and Gorefield.

Just before the church bear left, following the sign to Gorefield, and continue along the road to the Six Ringers' Inn, which gets its name from the six bells in the embattled tower of St Leonard's. Just past the pub turn left and follow Ringers' Lane. Turn right at the end of Ringers' Lane and follow the B1169 as far as Gadd's Lane. Turn left

On the walk

St Leonard's church

and follow Gadd's Lane, as it twists and turns, for about 1 mile. At the end of Gadd's Lane turn left and follow the road for about 150 yards.

② Turn left and follow the public footpath sign along the narrow, semi-metalled road (The Still) for approximately 1 mile, all the way back towards Leverington and the B1169. Turn left at the end of The Still, at the junction with the B1169 and follow the B1169 back to the Rising Sun.

PLACES OF INTEREST NEARBY

Elgood's Brewery in Wisbech, just off the A1101. Elgood and Sons Ltd have been producing beer at their Wisbech brewery at North Brink by the River Nene since 1795. The brewery has a visitors' centre and large, period-style gardens. Brewery tours are available by prior arrangement, telephone: 01945 583160. Also in North Brink is **Peckover House** (see Walk 4).

Helpston
The Blue Bell Inn

MAP: OS EXPLORER 235 (GR 121053)   **WALK 2**   **DISTANCE:** 3¾ MILES

DIRECTIONS TO START: FOLLOW THE A1 TO STAMFORD. FROM THE CENTRE OF STAMFORD FOLLOW SIGNS TO BURGHLEY HOUSE, WHICH IS LOCATED ON THE B1443. HOWEVER, INSTEAD OF TURNING OFF AT BURGHLEY HOUSE, CONTINUE FOLLOWING THE B1443 TO HELPSTON AND THE BLUE BELL INN. **PARKING:** IN THE PUB CAR PARK.

This walk gives you the chance to experience first-hand some of the countryside that inspired John Clare (1793–1864), one of England's most remarkable poets. He was born in the cottage next door to the Blue Bell Inn. If you're interested in reading some of his poetry, a good enough start would be *I Am!*, written during his last years. There are several websites devoted to him, and there is an annual John Clare festival held in the Blue Bell Inn (contact the pub for dates).

Much of this walk follows the route of the Torpel Way, which runs in its entirety between Bretton (on the western outskirts of Peterborough) and the eastern outskirts of Stamford. The Torpel Way links the villages between Peterborough and Stamford.

The Blue Bell Inn

This stone-built hostelry, which dates from the 17th century, has a traditional-looking bar area and a comfortable lounge with a large collection of teapots. There is a subtle and charming character to this pub, and a warm welcome on offer. With a bit of luck a visit to the Blue Bell Inn will coincide with one of the small-scale beer festivals they hold from time to time.

Opening hours are Monday to Friday, 11 am to 2 pm and 5 pm to 11 pm (flexible), Saturday from 11 am to 3 pm and 6 pm to 11 pm (flexible), Sunday from 12 noon to 4 pm and 7 pm to 10.30 pm. The beers served are Bateman's Best Bitter and XB, Hoskins Bitter and guest ales. Some bottled beers are also available.

Food times from Monday to Saturday are flexible, whilst Sunday lunch is served from 12.30 pm to 2 pm. Sunday lunch consists of two sittings, both of which are very popular and busy. It is therefore advisable to book in advance. Telephone: 01733 252394.

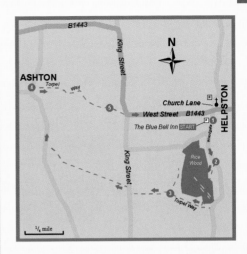

The Walk

① On leaving the pub turn right and follow the main road (Woodgate).

② Turn right, following the public footpath sign. Cross over a wooden stile and follow the grass track that runs immediately to the left-hand side of the hedgerow, to another wooden stile. Cross over this stile, following the yellow waymark arrow straight on along the narrow grass track through Rice Wood. The track runs straight for about 200 yards to the far edge of the trees, crossing over two other tracks (one of which is relatively wide) as it does so. Cross over a wooden stile as the woodland ends and follow the path directly on across a field for roughly 30 yards, to a public bridleway. Turn right onto the bridleway and follow the blue Torpel Way waymark arrow, keeping the ditch/beck to the immediate left-hand side.

③ Continue straight on at the wooden signpost (don't turn right), following the Torpel Way and King Street wooden signs. Keep the same ditch/beck to the immediate left-hand side and follow the bridleway to the main road (King Street). Turn right at King Street, following the wooden Torpel Way sign and yellow Torpel Way waymark arrow. Follow King Street for approximately 30 yards, then turn left at the public footpath sign and follow the broad dirt track for about $1/2$ mile to a wooden stile by a single-track metalled road. Cross over the stile, turn right and follow the road to Ashton.

④ Just beyond the road junction there is a

The fine memorial to the poet, John Clare

yellow Torpel Way waymark arrow directly across a field to a metal gateway, keeping just to the right of the electric power pylon. The metal gateway is a small, temporary structure and if by the time the walk is undertaken it has been removed, simply continue straight on towards a third wooden stile at the corner of the field. If the gateway is actually there, just pass through it and head towards the third wooden stile anyway. Once across this final wooden stile there is a road junction. Do not turn right or left here; instead, continue straight on in the same direction as before, following West Street (B1443) back to Helpston and the crossroads with Church Lane and Woodgate. At this crossroads you could turn left and follow Church Lane for a visit to the splendid Exeter Arms public house, or turn right along Woodgate, back to the Blue Bell Inn.

public footpath sign and a wooden Torpel Way sign. Turn right and follow these signs along a grass track. Stay with the grass track for about ²/₃ mile, keeping the hedgerow and ditch to the immediate left-hand side and, for most of the distance, a fence line to the immediate right-hand side.

⑤ Cross over the wooden stile and follow the yellow Torpel Way waymark arrow diagonally across a field to another wooden stile. Cross over this stile and follow the

PLACES OF INTEREST NEARBY

Burghley House, off the B1443, is roughly 1 mile east of Stamford. This magnificent country house was built between 1565 and 1587 by William Cecil, Lord High Treasurer of England. Remarkably, the house is a family home for his descendants to this day. Highlights of a visit to Burghley House include: David, 6th Marquis of Exeter, Lord Burghley's Olympic medals, Verrio's Heaven Room and Hell Staircase, the Sculpture Garden and a 160-acre deer park. The telephone number for visitor information, including opening times, is 01780 752451.

Orton Brimbles
The Granary

MAP: OS EXPLORER 227 (GR 154968)   **WALK 3**   **DISTANCE:** 4¾ MILES

DIRECTIONS TO START: TURN OFF THE A1 AT THE JUNCTION WITH THE A605, THEN FOLLOW THE A605 AND SIGNS TO NENE PARK. TURN LEFT FROM THE A605 AT THE SIGN FOR FERRY MEADOWS AND FOLLOW THIS MINOR ROAD TO HAM LANE. TURN RIGHT ONTO HAM LANE AND THE GRANARY IS ON THE LEFT. **PARKING:** IN THE PUB CAR PARK.

This walk mainly follows the River Nene and well defined paths within the 500-acre Ferry Meadows Country Park which lies at the heart of the 2,000 acre Nene Park. A number of water-based activities are on offer throughout the park, and a worthwhile canal boat trip leaves from the nearby Visitors' Centre. Look out for The Guardian, a sculpture with a story to tell.

The Granary

Part of the Beefeater chain of pubs, the Granary is built on several levels and with many snugs, which give it quite an intimate feeling. It has a farming theme and is decorated with many old agricultural implements. The beer is well kept and includes Boddingtons Bitter, Marston's Pedigree and Wadworth 6X. A selection of bottled ales is also available.

The pub is open all day on Monday to Saturday, from 11 am to 11 pm, and from 12 noon to 10.30 pm on Sunday. There is a large dining area where food – and there is a good choice – is served from 12 noon to 2 pm and from 5 pm to 10 pm on Monday to Thursday; 12 noon to 10 pm on Friday and Saturday; and all day on Sunday from 12 noon to 9 pm. Orton Meadows pitch and putt is virtually next door, should the mood to swing a golf club suddenly strike. Telephone: 01733 235794.

The Walk

① From the pub head to the road and turn right. Follow the road (Ham Lane) towards the Nene Valley Railway (Ferry Meadows Station). After about 150 yards there is a metalled cycle path. Follow this path towards Ferry Meadows in the same direction as before; the path runs parallel with Ham Lane and is marked by a blue cycle path sign. Rejoin Ham Lane just before the railway level-crossing. Follow Ham Lane over the level-crossing, then turn immediately right and follow the blue cycle path sign which points to the station, Orton Mere and city centre. Follow the metalled cycle path, as it runs parallel with the Nene Valley Railway, towards Orton Mere Station.

② Do not cross over the bridge, but bear right instead and continue along the metalled cycle path towards Orton Mere Station. After about 150 yards there is a railway level-crossing. Follow the cycle path over this level-crossing, then turn immediately left and follow the blue sign which points towards Orton Mere and city centre: the cycle path continues to run parallel with the Nene Valley Railway.

③ Bear left at the fork in the cycle path and continue on, in the direction of Orton Mere Station, to a T-junction. Turn left at the junction and follow the cycle path (marked by a blue cycle path sign which points to Thorpe Meadows and Longthorpe and Bretton) crossing first over a railway level-crossing and then Orton Lock and Sluices. Turn left just beyond the lock and follow the dirt track alongside the river bank (River Nene) for approximately 1 mile, to Bluebell Bridge. Turn right at the bridge (don't cross over it) and follow the metalled footpath for about 50 yards. After this short distance turn left and follow the wooden Riverside Walk sign

Looking west along the River Nene

along a dirt track. Riverside Walk runs for about ²/₃ mile, two sections of which are board-walked and tend to be slippery when wet, so take care. At the junction at the end of Riverside Walk, bear left and continue on along the dirt track, in roughly the same direction as before, to Ferry Bridge; essentially continuing to follow the course of the River Nene. Turn left at Ferry Bridge and cross over the river, then almost immediately turn left again and follow the metalled footpath back along the river for about 250 yards. Continue to follow the footpath after this distance as it bears right, away from the river. After another 200 yards or so the footpath comes to a junction. Bear left and continue following the footpath, keeping first Gunwade Lake and then Overton Lake to the right-hand side.

④ Follow the path round to the right and cross over the wooden bridge. On the other side of the bridge, follow the metalled footpath to the right and continue on along the shoreline of Overton Lake to the Visitors' Centre (where refreshments can be obtained). From the Visitors' Centre, follow the broad metalled path south, all the way back to Ham Lane and the Granary.

PLACES OF INTEREST NEARBY

The city of **Peterborough** is fabulous for shopping and looks new but is home to many cultural treasures. Highlights of a trip to Peterborough include the cathedral, built on the site of a Saxon abbey; Flag Fen, a 3,000 year old Bronze Age settlement just on the outskirts of the city; and Peterborough dog racing track, also just on the outskirts of the city (telephone: 01733 296939). Of course, the Nene Valley Railway is so close to the walk that it would almost be a shame not to take a trip on it. The telephone number for enquiries about the railway is 01780 784444. The telephone number for the Talking Timetable is 01780 784404.

Coates
The Vine

DIRECTIONS TO START: LEAVE THE A1 AT THE JUNCTION WITH THE A605. FOLLOW THE A605 EAST FOR ABOUT 10 MILES TO COATES. **PARKING:** IN THE PUB CAR PARK.

This delightful stroll in the Fens starts from the ancient village of Coates, with its magnificent village green, and visits the equally historic village of Eastrea. Both places date back to the Bronze Age and in fact, Eastrea has been permanently attached to the mainland only since the Fens were drained, about 300 years ago.

Our route follows rural bridleways and riverside pathways. After leaving behind Coates and Eastrea, the walk is wonderfully peaceful and quiet; the calm broken only by the sound of the occasional train.

The Vine

Situated in the heart of Coates village, the Vine has a large beer garden for use on warm days. There is frequent live entertainment here in the evening, including regular theme nights, bands and karaoke. The pub is open from 12 noon to 3 pm and 5 pm to 11 pm on Monday to Friday, all day on Saturday from 11 am to 11 pm, and from 11 am to 10.30 pm on Sunday.

Charles Wells Bombardier and Eagle are the beers on offer, along with guest ales, and bottled ales are also available. Food, which includes a varied bar snack menu, is served on Wednesday to Saturday, from 12 noon to 2 pm and from 5 pm to 9 pm. A roast lunch is also available on Sunday from 12 noon to 2.30 pm. There is no food available all day on Monday or at lunchtime on Tuesday but it is on offer from 5 pm to 9 pm on Tuesday evening. Telephone: 01733 840343.

The Walk

① On leaving the Vine cross over the A605 and follow the road along the edge of the village green, in the general direction of Holy Trinity church. Bear right at the junction by the church and continue on along a single-track metalled road. After about 150 yards there is a public bridleway sign and the road becomes a dirt track (Cow Way). Follow Cow Way, and after about ¹/₃ mile there is a modest crossroads. Continue straight on along Cow Way at this point; do not turn right onto Feldale Drove or left towards the houses. Cow Way ends at a residential area. Here the road is metalled and should be followed to the junction with

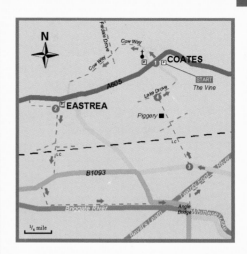

the A605. At the junction cross over the A605 and continue straight on, following the public byway sign along the dirt track that runs alongside the Nag's Head public house.

② Turn left at the junction by the public byway sign and continue along the dirt track to another junction. Turn left by the cycle route signs at this junction and follow the dirt track over the railway level-crossing; take care not to follow the cycle path round to the left at the junction just before the level-crossing. Once safely on the other side of the level-crossing, continue on along the (now grassy) dirt track to a metalled road (B1093). Turn right at the B1093 and follow the road to the first public footpath sign. Turn left at this sign and follow the dirt track to Briggate River. Turn left at the river and follow the riverside path for approximately 1 mile to the B1093. Turn right at the junction with the B1093 and follow the road towards Angle Bridge. Just before the bridge, turn left and follow the gravel track for approximately 10 yards to a wooden waymarker post. Turn

The Twenty Foot River

left at the post and follow the grass track to Twenty Foot River. Turn right at the river and follow the riverside path to a concrete bridge. Turn left and follow the single-track metalled road over the concrete bridge and continue on.

③ Turn right and follow the public footpath sign along a gravel track. Follow the gravel track dead straight for about 1 mile; eventually over a railway level-crossing and past a piggery.

④ Turn right at the junction, following the cycle path sign to Coates along a semi-metalled track (Lake Drove). After about 400 yards, at the bend by the houses, Lake Drove becomes a fully metalled road. Continue following this road, and the blue cycle path signs, into Coates, towards the A605 and back to the Vine.

PLACES OF INTEREST NEARBY

Peckover House, North Brink, Wisbech, just off the A1101, is a beautiful Georgian brickwork town house. It boasts a landscaped Victorian garden with herbaceous borders, roses, an orangery, a fernery and a summerhouse. Open between March and October, further details such as opening times and entrance fees, can be obtained by telephoning 01945 583463. Also in North Brink is **Elgood's Brewery** (see Walk 1).

Stilton
The Bell Inn

| MAP: OS EXPLORER 227 (GR 163892) | **WALK 5** | DISTANCE: 3¼ MILES |

DIRECTIONS TO START: LEAVE THE A1 AT THE JUNCTION WITH THE A15 (NORMAN CROSS) AND FROM THE ROUNDABOUT TAKE THE B1043 EXIT. FOLLOW THE B1043 AND CONTINUE INTO STILTON. THE BELL IS ON THE LEFT IN THE HIGH STREET. **PARKING:** ON THE ROADSIDE OUTSIDE THE BELL.

This walk is pleasantly rural, with hills and dips that take the rambler through Stilton and to the tiny hamlet of Denton. If you are lucky enough to be here during May Day Bank Holiday you may find yourself competing in the World Cheese Rolling Championship. This is held annually, on Stilton High Street.

The Bell Inn

The Bell is known as the birthplace of Stilton cheese, and it is indeed the very coaching inn from which the wonderful stuff was first sold all those years ago. The pub sign – an exact replica of the 16th-century original – is made of copper plate and the ornate bracket is wrought iron. This all adds up to an impressive combined weight of 2¾ tonnes. Famous visitors who have stayed at the Bell include the notorious highwayman Dick Turpin, Lord Byron and, relatively more recently, Clark Gable. The stone-floored Village Bar is open to non-residents and has a roaring log fire on chilly winter days.

Opening hours in the Village Bar are 12 noon to 2.30 pm and 6 pm to 11 pm on Monday to Friday, 12 noon to 3 pm and 6 pm to 11 pm on Saturday, and 12 noon to 3 pm and 7 pm to 10.30 pm on Sunday. The beers are Greene King Abbot Ale, Marston's Pedigree, Nethergate Suffolk Best Bitter and Oakham Ales Jeffrey Hudson Bitter. There is also a selection of bottled ales.

The Bell Inn has an award-winning and sumptuous restaurant offering modern British cuisine in 16th-century surroundings. Bar meals and snacks are also available in the Village Bar. Restaurant opening hours on Monday to Friday are 7 am to 9 am, 12 noon to 2 pm and 7 pm to 9.30 pm; on Saturday, 8 am to 9.30 am, 12 noon to 2 pm and 7 pm to 9.30 pm; whilst on Sunday they are 8 am to 9.30 am, 12 noon to 2 pm and 7 pm to 9 pm. If you want to stay longer in the area, accommodation is available here too. Telephone: 01733 241066.

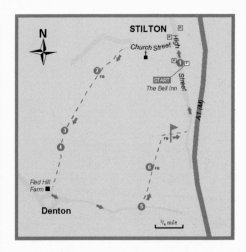

The Walk

① On leaving the Bell Inn turn right and follow the High Street to Church Street. Turn left and follow Church Street, past St Mary Magdalene church and on to a sharp right-hand bend in the road. Leave the road at this bend and follow the public footpath sign straight on along a single-track metalled road (which runs between the houses) for roughly 50 yards to a dirt/gravel track driveway. At the entrance to the driveway, follow the public footpath sign straight on towards a house. At the house, continue on the dirt track to the left, into the trees, and follow a yellow waymark arrow over a wooden stile. On the other side of the stile, follow the grass track across the field and up to another wooden stile. Cross over the wooden stile and follow the yellow waymark arrow straight on, across another field; take care at the stile, it crosses over an electrified fence!

② Pass through a gap in the hedgerow, crossing over a small wooden plank footbridge, and continue straight on across the field.

On the walk

(3) Pass by the end of the hedgerow, bear slightly left and follow the path down along a shallow gully towards the tallest copse of trees. Do not follow the paths to the left or the right at this junction.

(4) Cross over the wooden stile and continue on across the field to Red Hill Farm, Denton. At the farm, cross over the metal gate and continue along the public right of way through the small, narrow field, past the farmhouse and on to a single-track metalled road. Turn left and follow this road for about 100 yards to a junction. Bear left at the junction (do not turn right) and continue along the single-track metalled road (past the metal gate) for roughly $2/3$ mile.

(5) Turn left, cross over a wooden stile and follow the dirt/grass track for approximately $1/4$ mile, keeping the hedgerow to the right-hand side.

(6) At the corner of the field, pass through a gap in the hedgerow, climb over a wooden stile and follow the yellow waymark arrows across a wooden footbridge. On the other side of the footbridge, continue straight on for about 300 yards to a footpath junction, following the dirt track and keeping the hedgerow to the right-hand side. Turn right at the footpath junction, cross over a wooden footbridge and follow the fenced-off grass track to cut across the golf course, keeping the hedgerow to the left-hand side. After 300 yards or so, the grass track ends at a junction with a concrete path. Turn left at this junction and follow the public footpath sign along the concrete path towards Stilton. The concrete path ends at the start of the High Street. Follow the High Street all the way back to the Bell Inn.

PLACES OF INTEREST NEARBY

To the north-west of Stilton, **Elton Hall**, off the B671, close to the junction with the A605, is roughly 3 miles from the A1. It is an eclectic mix of Medieval, Gothic and Classical architectural styles and boasts wonderful furniture, Henry VIII's prayer book, paintings by many famous artists and beautiful gardens. Further information, including opening times, can be obtained by telephoning 01832 280468.

Sawtry
The Greystones

MAP: OS EXPLORER 227 (GR 167837)　　**WALK 6**　　**DISTANCE:** 5 MILES

DIRECTIONS TO START: THE EXIT FOR SAWTRY IS WELL SIGNPOSTED FROM THE A1(M). FOLLOW THIS EXIT INTO THE VILLAGE, THEN MAKE YOUR WAY TO THE CENTRE OF THE VILLAGE (THE GREEN) WHERE THE GREYSTONES IS SITUATED. **PARKING:** IN THE PUB CAR PARK.

Sawtry is a lively, industrious and pleasant village with two good pubs. The Green has traditionally been the centre of village life and until fairly recently, fairs were held there on feast days. The walk is easy to follow and leads across a gently rolling landscape and through ancient Aversley Wood which is now owned by the Woodland Trust.

The Greystones

This handsome, early 19th-century, Grade II listed building stands in the heart of Sawtry village. Its exterior is set in limestone and brick, while its interior displays wooden beams, which are adorned with decorative plates. There are also numerous miniature spirit bottles on display in wall-mounted glass cases. The Greystones has two bar areas, a snug and an enclosed beer garden.

The pub is open all day on Monday to Saturday from 10.30 am to 11 pm, and on Sunday from 12 noon to 3 pm and 7 pm to 10.30 pm. Beers on offer include Fuller's London Pride and Tetley's Bitter. The food is traditional pub fare, served in a friendly atmosphere. It is available at lunchtime throughout the week from 12 noon to 2 pm and in the evening on Monday to Saturday from 6 pm to 10.30 pm. Telephone: 01487 831999.

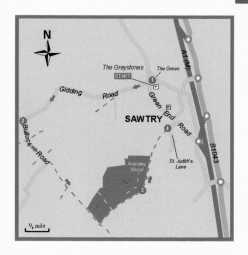

The Walk

① From the pub bear left and follow Gidding Road for approximately $1^1/2$ miles.

② Bear sharp left and continue to follow the metalled road (from the bend, Bullock Road). After about $^1/2$ mile there is a sharp right-hand bend. Leave the metalled road at this bend and continue straight ahead, following the public bridleway sign along a vehicle-rutted grass track. Follow the track towards the southern end of Aversley Wood, keeping the hedgerow/ditch to the immediate left-hand side. At the woods continue following the grass track along the south-west edge of the woods for approximately 50 yards to a metal gate and

a wooden stile. Turn left, cross over the stile and follow the grass track clearing, in a straight line, through the woods for about $^1/2$ mile. Aversley Wood is owned by the Woodland Trust, who kindly allow visitors free access; however, this does not imply an intention on their behalf to create a public right of way. About $^1/2$ mile along the track there is a junction with another grass track (Pinnacle Riding): about 50 yards or so before this junction the route starts to dip downhill. Turn right and follow Pinnacle Riding, in a more of less straight line, for $^1/3$ mile or so to the edge of the woodland.

③ At the edge of Aversley Wood there is a wooden gate. Pass through the gate to emerge at the corner of a field. Do not continue straight on or turn right at this point. Instead, turn left, passing though a small gap in the hedgerow, and follow a grass track alongside the edge of the woods, in the direction of Sawtry. Continue following the track alongside the woods, eventually over a wooden footbridge and on, up a hill, to the north-east corner of Aversley Wood. At the corner of the woodland, continue

Aversley Wood

straight on along the track, still in the direction of Sawtry. By now the grass track runs alongside a wire mesh, wooden post fence, and has done for about 200 yards since the wooden footbridge. After a further 200 yards or so, the fence ends and a hedgerow begins; although they are on opposite sides of the track. Continue straight ahead, keeping the hedgerow to the immediate left-hand side, following the track as it heads down into Sawtry.

④ Cross over the wooden stile and walk across the small, metalled car park to the bend in the road (St Judith's Lane). Do not turn right at the bend in the road, instead continue straight on to the junction with Green End Road. Turn left at this junction and follow Green End Road through Sawtry, all the way back to the Greystones; via the Bell public house, if the mood strikes.

PLACES OF INTEREST NEARBY
At Ramsey, to the east of Sawtry, **Ramsey Abbey**, is at the point where Chatteris Road leaves the B1096. Here you can see the remnants of a former Benedictine monastery, with a richly carved gatehouse. Open from April to October. Admission is free, but there is a donation box. Further information can be obtained by telephoning 01263 733471.

Purls Bridge
The Ship Inn

MAP: OS EXPLORER 228 (GR 477869) — WALK 7 — DISTANCE: 3½ MILES

DIRECTIONS TO START: FOLLOW THE A141 TO THE JUNCTION WITH THE B1093 AT WIMBLINGTON (APPROXIMATELY 2½ MILES SOUTH OF MARCH). FOLLOW THE B1093 INTO MANEA THEN TAKE A LEFT TURN ONTO A STRAIGHT ROAD WHICH SHOULD BE FOLLOWED TO THE JUNCTION WITH PURL'S BRIDGE DROVE. TURN LEFT ALONG PURL'S BRIDGE DROVE, ALL THE WAY TO THE SHIP INN. **PARKING:** IN THE PUB CAR PARK.

This is a wonderful walk for views: on a clear day you can see for many miles around. The route follows the straight course of the Old Bedford River for a short way. The area between the Old and New Bedford Rivers forms the Ouse Washes Nature Reserve. It is a bird and wildlife spotter's paradise, especially in the winter when the area floods. The reserve is really a ½ mile wide strip of permanent grassland which acts as a floodwater storage area, protecting the surrounding farmland from flooding.

The Ship Inn

This is a friendly locals' pub, very out of the way and off the beaten track. It may not look like the most beautiful pub in the world from the outside, but then looks can be deceptive. Inside it is well decorated and charmingly rustic, with a bit of a fishy theme. They keep a nice drop of ale too.

Opening hours: Monday to Tuesday, open on a casual basis in the summer. Wednesday to Saturday, 7 pm to 11 pm. Sunday, 12 noon until last afternoon customers leave and 7 pm to 11 pm (or noon to 11 pm if the afternoon customers don't leave). These opening times are subject to change, so it's probably best to ring in advance just to make sure.

The beers are Castle Eden Ale and Flowers IPA, together with guest ales. Some bottled ales are also available. Food is served whenever the pub is open, and comes in generous and tasty helpings. Telephone: 01354 680578.

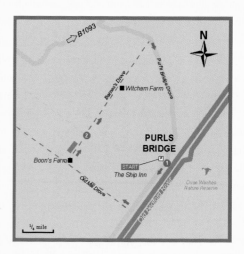

The Walk

① From the pub turn right and follow the single-track metalled road for about ¹/₂ mile to a public bridleway sign, alongside the Old Bedford River. Turn right at the public bridleway sign and follow the raised, vehicle-rutted dirt track (Old Mill Drove) to Boon's Farm (a small collection of old farm buildings). Turn right at the junction by Boon's Farm, then follow the gravel

Farmland near Purl's Bridge Drove

En route

track (Barnes's Drove) in the direcion of Manea.

② Bear right at the fork in the gravel track and continue on along Barnes's Drove in the same direction as before, ie towards Manea. At this fork in the track there is a well tended and isolated garden with many different varieties of plants. Why? Who knows? After approximately 1 mile Barnes's Drove comes to a junction with a single-track metalled road (Purl's Bridge Drove). Turn right and follow this road back to the Ship Inn.

PLACES OF INTEREST NEARBY

Ouse Washes Nature Reserve, just over the Old Bedford River from Purls Bridge and signed from Manea village. The reserve provides the visitor with an excellent introduction to the wildlife of the Fens. During the winter, the reserve floods, attracting ducks and swans making it in fact the most important site in Britain for wintering ducks and swans. During the summer, breeding birds such as redshanks, lapwings and snipe can be seen. There is a visitors' centre, open daily from 9 am to 5 pm (except 25th and 26th December). The reserve is managed by the RSPB (telephone 01603 660066) and the Wildlife Trust (telephone 01223 712400).

Witcham
The White Horse Inn

MAP: OS EXPLORER 228 (GR 462799)	**WALK 8**	**DISTANCE:** 3 MILES

DIRECTIONS TO START: WITCHAM IS REACHED ON THE A142 BETWEEN CHATTERIS AND ELY. THE SLADE IS THE MAIN ROAD THAT LEADS OFF THE A142 INTO WITCHAM, AND THE WHITE HORSE INN IS LOCATED OFF THE SLADE ON SILVER STREET. **PARKING:** IN THE PUB CAR PARK.

Leafy country lanes and hedge-lined grass tracks are followed for most of the length of this walk. There are also good views of the Fens and the villages to the north-west of Ely. Part of the route follows a short section of Catchwater Drain, one of the many fenland watercourses that keep the Fens from becoming boggy and marshy. The village of Witcham has been inhabited for over 6,000 years. The village sign was donated by the Women's Institute to mark Queen Elizabeth II's Silver Jubilee. The fire engine depicted on it was used only once, to put out a fire at Smith's Barn. The engine currently resides in Ely Museum.

The White Horse Inn

The decor in the White Horse Inn is modern, wooden and rustic. That doesn't sound like much, but it is. The floor is part tiled, part carpeted, the bar counter is wood panelled and there is a separate dining area and carvery. There is also a small landscaped beer garden. The bar right by the entrance-way to the pub fills up very quickly, but there is usually more room to spread out further inside.

Opening hours are evenings only on Monday and Tuesday, from 6.30 pm to 11 pm; Wednesday to Friday, 12 noon to 3 pm and 6.30 pm to 11 pm; Saturday and Sunday 12 noon to 3 pm (or until the last customer leaves) and 6.30 pm to 11 pm (unless the last customer doesn't leave).

The beer is Adnams Bitter and there are several guest ales. A selection of bottled beers is also available. Tasty and well prepared bar meals are served on Wednesday to Saturday, from 12 noon to 2.30 pm or thereabouts and from 6.30 pm to 9 pm. A carvery is on offer at Sunday lunchtime from 12 noon to 2.30 pm or thereabouts. Telephone: 01353 778298.

The Walk

① From the pub turn right and follow Silver Street to the crossroads with The Slade and the High Street. Turn left at the crossroads and follow The Slade up a gentle hill.

② Turn right at the public byway sign and follow the broad, vehicle-rutted grass track (Bury Road) to the junction with Wardy Hill Road. At this junction turn left and follow the public byway sign along Wardy

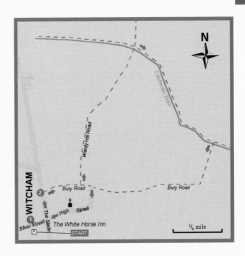

Hill Road (a broad, vehicle-rutted dirt track). Two tracks run in the same direction at this junction. Only the first path, marked by the public byway sign and which runs between two hedgerows, is the public right of way. After about ³/₄ mile Wardy Hill Road comes to a crossroads. Turn right here and follow the broad dirt track, keeping Catchwater Drain to the immediate right-hand side. The first junction occurs approximately ³/₄ mile along the dirt track. Turn right at this junction and follow a narrower dirt/grass track (Bury Road

Bury Road

again) which runs between two treelines/hedgerows. At the junction by several old farm buildings Bury Road becomes a single-track gravel road. At this point continue straight on along Bury Road towards Witcham. At a junction roughly ⅓ mile further on, Bury Road becomes a single-track metalled road. Turn left at this junction and follow Headley's Lane to the T-junction with the High Street. Follow the High Street back to the crossroads with The Slade and Silver Street, and finally follow Silver Street back to the White Horse Inn.

Ely
The Cutter Inn

MAP: OS EXPLORER 226 (GR 545797) · **WALK 9** · **DISTANCE:** 3¼ MILES

DIRECTIONS TO START: FOLLOW THE A142 TO ELY AND THE ROUNDABOUT WITH
STATION ROAD. ALMOST IMMEDIATELY AFTER TURNING OFF NORTHWARDS ONTO
STATION ROAD, TURN RIGHT AND FOLLOW ANNESDALE TO THE CUTTER INN. **PARKING:**
IN THE PUB CAR PARK. IF IT IS FULL THERE IS AMPLE FREE PARKING ON THE
SURROUNDING ROADS OR IN THE MANY CAR PARKS LOCATED THROUGHOUT ELY.

This walk is a good excuse to stroll along the River Great Ouse and to explore the beautiful and historic city of Ely. Do not miss the opportunity to visit the magnificent Norman Cathedral. Steeped in history, Ely also has a wealth of good pubs, several of which are passed en route. So you can combine a leisurely amble to see the wildlife on the river with some sightseeing, knowing that refreshments are ever close at hand.

The Cutter Inn

Scenically positioned on the riverside, the name of the Cutter Inn is derived from the river diversion ('cut') that brought the Great Ouse nearer to Ely. The pub is divided in two, one half is the bar, the other the dining room. There is dark wood panelling throughout, a large brick fireplace and an excellent waterside view from the bar. Watch out for the stuffed eel, it's a whopper.

The pub is open from 11 am every day, to 11 pm on Monday to Saturday and to 10.30 pm on Sunday. The beers served are Greene King IPA, John Smith's Bitter, Morland Old Speckled Hen, plus bottled ales. A separate and cosy dining room serves a wide and tasty selection of food – the home-made pies are particularly good. Food is available throughout the week from 12 noon to 2.30 pm and from 6.30 pm to 9.30 pm. The pub can be busy at the weekends, so it's probably advisable to book in advance. Telephone: 01353 662713.

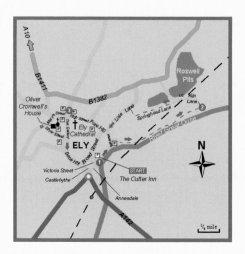

The Walk

① From the pub turn left and follow the riverside towpath along the Fen Rivers Way. Keep to the riverside as closely as possible, for about 1¹/₂ miles, following Fen Rivers Way waymark arrows.

② Pass through the wooden gate, bear left and follow the narrow, metalled footpath, yellow waymark arrow and the Black Fen Waterway Trail small black waymark arrow. The footpath passes by some industrial buildings and continues to Kiln Lane. At Kiln Lane, turn left and follow the road over the railway level-crossing. Immediately

on the other side of the level-crossing turn left, following the public footpath sign pointing to the Hereward Way and a narrow metalled footpath (Springhead Lane). Springhead Lane is metalled as far as the trees (roughly 50 yards), after which time it becomes a dirt track leading through the trees. At the end of Springhead Lane (roughly ¹/₃ mile), pass through a wooden gate, following a yellow waymark arrow to continue the final 10 yards or so to the main road (Lisle Lane). Turn left and follow Lisle Lane until it terminates at the

PLACES OF INTEREST NEARBY

Ely Cathedral – vast, impressive and unmissable since the early 1080s. **Oliver Cromwell's House**, next to St Mary's church on St Mary's Street, where you can see how this infamous republication and Puritan lived in the mid-17th century. The walk passes by both attractions. If you would like a longer stay in this lovely city, there is a wide variety of accommodation available in and around Ely. For the latest information, contact the Tourist Information Centre, Oliver Cromwell's House, 29 St Mary's Street, Ely, CB7 4HF; telephone: 01353 662062.

The war memorial in High Street, Ely

T-junction with Waterside and Fore Hill. Turn right at the T-junction and follow Fore Hill up the hill, straight on past the junction with Broad Street, and on to the High Street. Follow the High Street to the slightly staggered crossroads with St Mary's Street and The Gallery. At this point the walk can be interrupted in order to visit Ely Cathedral (The Gallery) or any of the three pubs that cluster around the crossroads.

③ To resume the walk, set off from the crossroads along St Mary's Street; eventu-ally leading past Oliver Cromwell's house and on to Silver Street. Turn left at Silver Street and continue to the junction with The Gallery. Turn right onto The Gallery; but not immediately right onto the small road that connects with Barton Road. Continue on along The Gallery as it becomes Back Hill, then follow Back Hill for about 300 yards down to Castlehythe. Turn left and follow Castlehythe to Annesdale (roughly 50 yards), then turn left and follow Annesdale back to the Cutter Inn.

Earith
The Riverview Hotel

MAP: OS EXPLORER 225 (GR 387748)   **WALK 10**   **DISTANCE:** 4¼ MILES

DIRECTIONS TO START: THE RIVERVIEW HOTEL IS SITUATED TOWARDS
THE SOUTH-EAST OF EARITH ON THE A1123. **PARKING:** IN THE PUB CAR PARK.

The going is flat, and the walk leads between the three villages of Earith, Colne (pronounced 'Cone') and Bluntisham. Earith is situated just to the west of the Old and New Bedford Rivers, on the northerly bank of the River Great Ouse. The Bedford Rivers are two of the main drainage channels for the Fens, and were dug out in 1631 and 1651. Between lies The Hundred Foot Washes, which flood in the winter and are home to a variety of water fowl.

The Riverview Hotel

A visit to this picturesque 16th-century coaching inn is a comfortable and friendly experience. Outside there is a riverside beer garden and inside there are wood-beam ceilings and wood-panelled bars. Look out for the stag.

Opening hours are 12 noon to 3 pm and 5 pm to 11 pm on Monday to Friday and 12 noon to 3 pm and 6 pm to 11 pm on Saturday; Sunday hours are 12 noon to 3 pm and 7 pm to 11 pm. The beer is Greene King IPA, plus a variety of bottled ales. There is a large and comfortable dining room, separate from the main bar. An à la carte menu is offered, with food served in the dining room and the bar area. A full roast lunch can be enjoyed on Sundays. Food is available all week from 12 noon to 2.30 pm and from 6 pm to 9.30 pm but it can be busy at the weekends, so it's best to book in advance. The Riverview Hotel also provides accommodation. Telephone: 01487 841405.

The Walk

① From the Riverview Hotel turn left and follow the main road (A1123) towards the bridge across the Old Bedford River. Just before the bridge turn left, cross over the wooden stile and follow the public footpath sign along the riverside grass track. After about ½ mile of following the track beside the river turn left, pass through a double gate and continue on to a road junction. At the junction, turn right and follow the met-alled road to a dirt track, at which point continue straight on, past the fishing ponds, to the junction with Holme Drove. Turn left at the junction and follow Holme

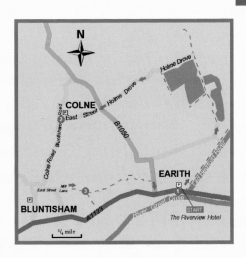

Drove to Colne and the crossroads with the B1050 and East Street. Continue straight on at the crossroads, following East Street to the junction with Bluntisham Road. If time permits, pop into the Green Man public house at this junction.

② Follow Bluntisham Road (which eventually becomes Colne Road) to Bluntisham and the junction of Colne Road and East Street (another one). One option at this junction is to turn right and follow East Street the 40 or so yards to the White Swan public house. The second option is to miss a visit to this pub and turn left at the junction. Either way, the walk continues by following East Street east in the general direction of Earith. At the junction with Mill Lane, East Street bends off to the right. Leave East Street at this junction and continue on along Mill Lane in the same direction as before.

③ Climb over the gate, bear left at the fork in the grass track and cross over the field (approximately 100 yards) to a gap in the hedgerow opposite. At the gap follow

One of the fine pubs that can be visited on the walk

the track straight on to a junction. At the junction, follow the narrower grass track to the left. Do not follow the grass track to the right; although broader and well used, it is not a public right of way. The narrower grass track eventually leads to a junction Turn left here and follow the track around the barbed-wire-topped fence to a wooden stile. Cross over the stile and follow the track straight on to a kissing-gate; keeping the fence line and buildings to the right-hand side. Pass through the kissing-gate and continue straight on towards the junction with the main road (B1050). Turn

right at this junction and follow the B1050 to the junction with the A1123. Turn left and follow the A1123 back to the Riverview Hotel.

PLACES OF INTEREST NEARBY

The Raptor Foundation, off the B1086, 1¾ miles north-east of St Ives and west of Earith via Bluntisham, is a bird of prey rescue centre giving regular flying displays. Open all year round for a face-to-beak close encounter of the feathered variety. Telephone: 01487 741140.

Catworth
The Racehorse Inn

MAP: OS EXPLORER 225 (GR 085732) | **WALK 11** | **DISTANCE:** 5¼ MILES

DIRECTIONS TO START: TURN OFF THE A14 AT THE JUNCTION WITH THE B660, THEN FOLLOW THE B660 SOUTH FOR ABOUT 1¼ MILES TO CATWORTH VILLAGE AND THE RACEHORSE INN. **PARKING:** IN THE PUB CAR PARK.

This walk is mainly along rural lanes and quiet country roads; on clear days the views of the encompassing rolling hills are magnificent. There are shorter routes that could have been followed in the immediate area around Catworth, but none of the relevant paths were very well kept or well marked at the time of writing. Surrounded on all sides by farmland, Catworth is a quiet village and just up the road from Huntingdon racecourse. Its 13th-century church, St Leonard's, possesses an octagonal spire and contains a monument to Rose Dryden (sister of the poet, John Dryden).

The Racehorse Inn

As you might expect in a pub named the Racehorse Inn, there is a decidedly equine flavour to the interior. The walls are adorned with paintings and pictures that pay homage to the noble sport of horse racing, and the equine theme is reinforced further by the presence of that almost obligatory item of rural pub décor, horse brasses. They even have a map showing the location of all the racecourses in Britain and Ireland. However, do not despair if you're not a horse racing fan, the Racehorse is still a friendly and inviting place, with its wood beams, wooden flooring and, best of all in the colder months, open fire. Chess and bridge nights are also held.

Opening hours are 11.30 am to 3 pm and 6 pm to 11 pm on Monday to Friday; on Saturday and Sunday it is open all day from 11.30 am to 11 pm. Beers on offer are Adnams Bitter, Marston's Pedigree, John Smith's Bitter, Theakston Best Bitter and Wadworth 6X. Bottled ales are also available. For food there is a choice between dining in the main pub or the pleasant and separate dining area. It is served from 11.30 am to 2 pm and 6 pm to 9 pm on Monday to Friday, and from 11.30 am to 3 pm and 6 pm to 9 pm on Saturday and Sunday. Food serving hours are flexible for larger group bookings. Telephone: 01832 710262.

The Walk

① From the pub turn left and follow the single track metalled road down towards Brook End Farm.

② Pass through the gate and follow the

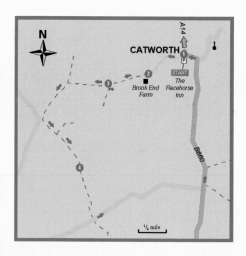

public bridleway sign along the gravel track. After about 20 yards bear right (at the junction by Brook End Farm) and continue along the bridleway to a sharp right-hand bend in the gravel track. At the bend (marked by a private road sign), turn left and follow the bridleway (now a grass track) alongside a hedgerow, keeping the hedgerow to the left-hand side. It is possible to leave the gravel track slightly sooner, but following the large bridlepath sign (it can't be missed), regardless of anything else, will point out the correct route.

③ Walk past the wooden footbridge and continue on to the junction of the grass and gravel tracks. Continue straight on at the junction, following the bridlepath sign and keeping the hedgerow to the left-hand side; do not turn left or right onto the gravel tracks marked as private roads. After roughly ⅓ mile there is a junction at the corner of the field. Turn left here, passing through a wide gap at the end of the hedgerow, then follow the track as it runs alongside the field edge, keeping another hedgerow to the right-hand side. The track

Catworth is surrounded on all sides by gentle farmland

eventually leads to a junction with a single track metalled road, and close to this junction there is a wooden gate. Pass through the gate and follow the public bridleway sign to turn left and follow a grass track alongside the field edge (keeping its hedgerow to the right-hand side).

④ At the corner of the field, pass through a gap in the hedgerow and continue on through an old brick culvert of a long dismantled railway. On the other side of the culvert, continue straight on along the bridleway, following a grass track alongside a field edge and keeping a hedgerow to the left-hand side. The track leads straight on through two hedgerow gaps (ie along the edge of three adjoining fields) and eventually, via a quick jink, to a single track metalled road. Turn left at the road and follow it to a junction with the B660. Turn left at the junction and follow the B660 all the way back to Catworth and the Racehorse Inn.

PLACES OF INTEREST NEARBY

Bushmead Priory at Colmworth is a medieval refectory of an Augustinian priory founded in 1195. It has a 13th-century timber roof, medieval wall paintings and stained glass windows. Admission is free, and more information can be obtained by telephone: 01234 376614.

Brampton
Brampton Mill

MAP: OS EXPLORER 225 (GR 225706)

WALK 12

DISTANCE: 2 MILES

DIRECTIONS TO START: FOLLOW THE A1 TO THE JUNCTION WITH THE A14. AT THIS ROUNDABOUT GO EAST ON THE A14 TOWARDS HUNTINGDON. TAKE THE FIRST EXIT OFF THE A14, FOLLOWING THE SIGNS TO BRAMPTON AND THE RACECOURSE, AND FOLLOW THE B1514 TOWARDS HUNTINGDON. CONTINUE PAST TWO ROUNDABOUTS. ABOUT ½ MILE FROM THE SECOND ROUNDABOUT TURN RIGHT, ONTO BROMHOLME LANE; THE ENTRANCE TO THIS NARROW ROAD IS MARKED WITH A SIGN FOR BRAMPTON MILL. **PARKING:** IN THE PUB CAR PARK.

This circuit is short and easy, and takes the walker down quiet lanes, along riverside paths, across a golf course and through a scenic churchyard in the village of Brampton. Brampton's most famous former inhabitant is undoubtedly the 17th-century diarist Samuel Pepys.

Pepys lived in Brampton for part of his boyhood and attended Huntingdon Free School (now Hinchingbrooke School). He often referred to Brampton and Hinchingbrooke in his diaries. The house he inherited from his uncle, and where he used to live, can be seen on the route.

Brampton Mill

Brampton Mill, previously known as the Olde Mill, was formerly owned by the Beefeater chain of pub/restaurants. In 2000 it was bought, renamed and made-over by the Out and Out chain, and the resulting decor, with its emphasis on wood panelling and pale colours, is clean and light. The bar area has stone flooring and a low, wooden-beamed ceiling; remember, duck or grouse. Brampton Mill is idyllically situated on a bank of the River Great Ouse. It also has a rotating water wheel. The Domesday Book records the presence of a mill at this location.

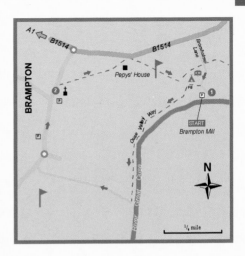

The opening hours throughout the week are 12 noon to 11 pm. Charles Wells Bombardier, Wadworth 6X and Marston's Pedigree are the beers available, along with various bottled ales. There is also a good selection of wines. The large restaurant area is open every day from 12 noon to 2.30 pm and 6 pm to 9.30 pm. It tends to be especially busy at weekends, so it's advisable to book in advance. Bar snacks are available daily from 12 noon to 11 pm, and tea, speciality coffees and hot chocolate are served too. Telephone: 01480 459758.

The Walk

① From Brampton Mill turn left and follow Bromholme Lane for roughly 100 yards. Turn left and follow the public footpath/Ouse Valley Way sign and yellow Ouse Valley Way waymark arrows. The path soon bears left and leads to a small concrete footbridge. Follow the path over this footbridge, and continue to follow the yellow Ouse Valley Way waymark arrows as the path leads down to and along the riverside (approximately ½ mile). At the first junction turn right and follow the path past the sewage works (not as smelly as it sounds) towards the main road. Turn right at the main road, then cross over the roundabout at the entrance to RAF Brampton and continue on towards St Mary Magdalene church.

PLACES OF INTEREST NEARBY

Hinchingbrooke House and **Hinchingbrooke Country Park** are off the B1514, just north of Brampton. The historic country house, now a school, is open to the public in the summer months on Sunday afternoons, telephone 01480 375678. The park, spread over 156 acres, has walks, abundant wildlife, a life size reproduction of an Iron Age settlement and many open-air musical and theatrical events in the summer. There is also a lake with a water sports centre. Further information on Hinchingbrooke Country Park can be obtained by telephone: 01480 451568.

Nearby is **Huntingdon Race Course**, off the junction of the A14 and B1514 and approximately ½ mile to the north of Brampton. General information, including the schedule of race meetings, is obtainable by telephone, 01480 453373.

The marina opposite Brampton Mill

② Turn right at the entrance to the 13th-century parish church of St Mary Magdalene, Brampton. Walk through the church grounds (keeping to the left) towards a kissing-gate. Follow the public footpath sign at the wooden kissing-gate; the path leads to the B1514 via two more wooden kissing-gates. Pass through another wooden kissing-gate just before the B1514, then turn immediately right and follow the public footpath sign towards Huntingdon and Godmanchester. Just before you take this path take a quick glance at the house just to the right, this is the house once owned by Samuel Pepys. The path to Huntingdon and Godmanchester leads to yet another wooden kissing-gate, then through a golf course, where blue right-of-way marker posts should be followed. The golf course is popular and usually busy, especially at the weekends, so please be careful of flying golf balls. The path across the golf course leads to a wooden kissing-gate. Pass through the kissing-gate, keep left, and follow the path straight ahead, through a caravan park, to Bromholme Lane. Turn right at Bromholme Lane and follow the path back to the pub.

Buckden
The Lion Hotel

MAP: OS EXPLORER 225 (GR 191676) | **WALK 13** | **DISTANCE:** 2½ MILES

DIRECTIONS TO START: FOLLOW THE A1 TO THE BUCKDEN ROUNDABOUT (BETWEEN ST NEOTS AND HUNTINGDON, AT THE JUNCTION WITH THE B661) AND TURN OFF INTO BUCKDEN HIGH STREET. **PARKING:** ON THE ROADSIDE OUTSIDE THE LION HOTEL.

This stroll is very easy, following metalled roads all the way round, and takes the walker through Buckden village and its immediate surrounding countryside. Buckden Palace, located in the middle of the village, was the residence of the Bishops of Lincoln between 1186 and 1838. It was also once the prison for Catherine of Aragon, first wife of Henry VIII. The Queen's Tower is now reduced to its foundations but the King's Tower is a fine example of a Tudor building. The Queen Katherine garden is a recent restoration in the grounds of the palace, using authentic Tudor and pre-Tudor plants.

The Lion Hotel

Very little is recorded about the history or owners of this 15th-century, Grade II listed building, but like all 'good' historical buildings there are many tales of a resident ghost. Known as the 'Lady in Grey', and apparently accompanied by the smell of lavender, she has been seen by many very rational people. It is said that the ghost may be linked to an accident where a young woman was crushed to death by a coach drawing through the narrow entrance archway. The Lion Hotel was probably originally built as a guest house for the Bishop of Lincoln's Palace in about 1492. However, many of the timbers in the Great Hall are thought to be much older. This room, now the bar and lounge, still retains its original 15th-century fireplace, complete with carved Tudor rose. The five-spoke ceiling has a carved central boss showing the Lamb & Papal pennant with the words *Ecce Agnus Dei*, which translates as 'Behold the Lamb of God'. The hotel has variously been called the Lamb, the Lamb & Flag and the Lion & Lamb. There have been many alterations over the years, including a Georgian wing. The present bar was once the village butcher's shop.

The opening hours are 12 noon to 3.30 pm and 6 pm to 11 pm every day. Greene King IPA and Ruddles County are the beers on offer, alongside some bottled ales and a good selection of wines. There is a large restaurant with an impressive menu, or you can opt for a bar snack from a varied list. Food is served from 12 noon to 2 pm and from 7 pm to 9 pm each day. Overnight accommodation is also available at the hotel. Telephone: 01480 810313.

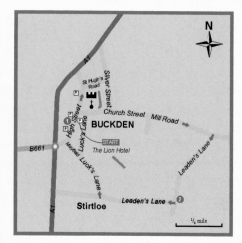

The Walk

① From the Lion Hotel turn right and follow the High Street through the village, past Buckden Palace, to St Hugh's Road. Turn right at St Hugh's Road and continue all the way to its end and the T-junction with Silver Street. Turn right at Silver

The approach to Stirtloe village

Buckden Palace

Street and follow it to the T-junction with Church Street. Turn left at Church Street and continue on. Eventually Church Street becomes Mill Road. However, despite the two names it is all one road, and should be followed out of the village to Leaden's Lane. At Leaden's Lane turn right, following the sign to Stirtloe, and continue on.

② Bear sharp right and continue along Leaden's Lane towards Stirtloe and the T-junction with Luck's Lane. Turn right at Luck's Lane and follow the sign to Buckden. Closer to Buckden, Luck's Lane becomes Mayfield. At this point continue

> **PLACES OF INTEREST NEARBY**
> **Grafham Water**, off the B661, approximately 1 mile to the west of Buckden, was the largest reservoir in England when it opened in the mid-1960s. Diverse wildlife habitats were included in the original design and now support a variety of wildlife. Water sports, cycling, walking and fishing can all be enjoyed here. For further information, contact the Grafham Water Visitors' Centre, telephone 01480 812154.

straight on along Mayfield to the High Street. Turn right at the High Street and continue back to the Lion Hotel.

Houghton
The Three Horseshoes

MAP: OS EXPLORER 225 (GR 281722) | **WALK 14** | **DISTANCE:** 2¾ MILES

DIRECTIONS TO START: HOUGHTON IS LOCATED MIDWAY BETWEEN HUNTINGDON AND ST IVES, JUST TO THE SOUTH OF THE A1123. FOLLOW THE TURN OFF TO HOUGHTON OR WYTON, AND THE ROAD WILL LEAD TO THE THREE HORSESHOES. **PARKING:** IN THE PUB CAR PARK.

This mainly riverside walk follows the River Great Ouse as it twists and turns to the south of Houghton village. Houghton and its twin to the west, Wyton, are really one single expanse of village; even the locals aren't sure where Houghton ends and Wyton begins. Houghton's best known landmark is Houghton Mill, one of the last and most complete left standing on the Great Ouse. The village's celebrated miller was Potto Brown, a Victorian philanthropist and Nonconformist. He was a proponent of temperance and a committed religious man, so heaven knows what he'd make of his mention in a *Pub Strolls* book. His bust has stood in Houghton since its unveiling in 1879.

The Three Horseshoes

This is a long and low 17th-century building, with a pantiled roof. Inside it is comfortable, welcoming and friendly. The Three Horseshoes is open all day on Monday to Saturday from 11 am to 11 pm and on Sunday from 12 noon to 10.30 pm. Beers on offer are Greene King Abbot Ale and IPA. Bottled ales are also available. Bar snacks can be ordered throughout the day and there is a separate dining area where food is served all week from 12 noon to 2 pm and from 7 pm to 9 pm. Telephone: 01480 462410.

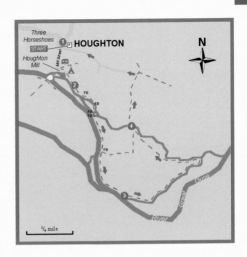

The Walk

① From the pub follow Mill Street towards Houghton Mill. Roughly 20 yards or so before the mill, turn left and pass through a gate by a sign for Houghton Mill Water Close Meadow; this is the entrance to a caravan and camping park. After about 10 yards, and just beyond the tearooms, there is a junction. Follow the gravel path and plain yellow waymark arrow to the right at this junction; do not follow the yellow Ouse Valley Way waymark arrow to the left. After another 10 yards or so, leave the gravel path and bear right to follow the grass track along the riverside. Follow all the subsequent yellow waymark arrows along the riverside grass track.

② Pass through the kissing-gate and walk across the field to a wooden footbridge. Cross over the footbridge and continue on along the grass track for about 25 yards, bearing right to another wooden footbridge. Cross over this footbridge and follow the yellow waymark arrow straight on across the field to a small weir. Cross over the wooden footbridge at the weir and continue straight on for another 10 yards or so to another wooden footbridge over another small weir. After crossing over the second weir, continue straight on along the riverside grass track.

Houghton's famous miller

Houghton Mill

③ Do not cross over the concrete footbridge at the weir. Instead, continue on for about 10 yards to a wooden stile. Cross over the stile, and another wooden stile about 5 yards further on, then follow the yellow waymark arrows along the riverside grass track.

④ Pass through the wooden kissing-gate, or cross over the adjacent wooden stile (depending on who your walking partner is), then cross over the concrete bridge and continue on along the gravel track for about ¹/₄ mile to a junction. Turn left at the junction and follow the single track metalled road for just over ¹/₄ mile to another junction. Do not turn left at the junction. Instead, bear slightly right and continue following the single track metalled road all the way back to the Three Horseshoes.

> **PLACES OF INTEREST NEARBY**
> **Houghton Mill**, Houghton, the last working water mill on the River Great Ouse, is open from March until October. Opening times, entrance charges and other information can be obtained by telephone: 01480 301494. There is even stone-ground wholemeal flour for sale.

Fenstanton
The King William IV

MAP: OS EXPLORER 225 (GR 314685) | **WALK 15** | **DISTANCE:** 2¾ MILES

DIRECTIONS TO START: FENSTANTON IS JUST OFF THE A14, MIDWAY BETWEEN CAMBRIDGE AND HUNTINGDON. FOLLOW THE SIGNED SLIP ROAD OFF THE A14 TO THE VILLAGE. THE KING WILLIAM IV IS SITUATED AT THE WESTERN END OF THE HIGH STREET.
PARKING: IN THE PUB CAR PARK.

The walk follows metalled roads through Fenstanton and well-used paths across farmland and along a short stretch of the River Great Ouse. Fenstanton's great claim to fame is that Lancelot 'Capability' Brown was once the Lord of the Manor. 'Capability' Brown, the famed landscape gardener, laid out many large gardens, including Kew and Blenheim. He and his wife are buried in the village churchyard. Fenstanton retains many buildings from the Georgian period, including the clock tower (built around 1650 and restored in 1989) which started out as a village lock-up.

The King William IV

Known to the locals as 'the King Bill,' the King William IV was originally two cottages, dating from the 16th and 17th centuries. In its first incarnation it was a 'parlour' pub, brewing its own beer in the half-octagonal section of the building. It has low-beamed ceilings throughout and a large, brick, log-burning fireplace which stands in the middle of the building. The fireplace divides the bars and the restaurant area, and also indicates the division between the original two cottages.

The opening hours on Monday to Saturday are 11 am to 3.30 pm and 6 pm to 11 pm and on Sunday the pub is open all day from 12 noon to 11 pm. Live music is presented most Wednesday evenings, mainly jazz, blues and rock. Beers are Greene King Abbot Ale and IPA, Ruddles County and Badger Tanglefoot, and there are bottled ales too. Hot and cold bar food is available and most appetites are catered for with dishes ranging from a three-cheese ploughman's lunch to the King William IV's renowned steak and kidney pudding. Daily specials and vegetarian options are also on offer. Food is served every day between 12 noon and 2.15 pm and on Monday to Saturday from 7 pm to 10 pm. B & B is available here, all rooms en-suite. Telephone: 01480 462467.

The Walk

① From the King William IV cross over the road and follow Chequer Street straight ahead to Hall Green Lane. Turn left at Hall Green Lane and continue on towards a kissing-gate. Pass through the kissing-

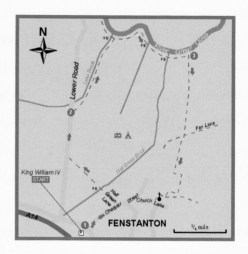

gate and continue along the dirt track, which runs between hedgerows, towards a wooden footbridge. Cross over the footbridge and follow the pathway straight on, past the cricket field, towards Lower Road. Turn right along Lower Road.

② After approximately ¼ mile turn right, cross over the wooden stile and follow the public footpath sign and yellow waymark arrow along a dirt track. Stay on this pathway to the River Great Ouse, keeping Lake Brook (no more than a ditch) to the left-hand side. Halfway to the river there is a gate and stile. Cross over this stile, following the white Huntingdonshire Country Walks waymark arrow, and continue along the same pathway. Halfway to the river from this stile there is another one, cross over this second stile, again following the white Huntingdonshire Country Walks waymark arrow, and again continue along the same pathway towards the river. At the wooden footbridge follow the Harcamlow Way waymark arrow to the right and head east along the southerly bank of the River Great Ouse. This path

The River Great Ouse looking towards St Ives

eventually crosses over a metal footbridge (where the Harcamlow Way and yellow waymark arrows should be followed straight on), then crosses over a concrete footbridge (where the black 'Permissive Way' waymark arrow should be ignored, as it isn't a public right of way).

③ Turn right and follow the yellow waymark arrow straight across the field, following the public right of way back towards Fenstanton. Turn right at the junction with Fen Lane, following the Harcamlow Way waymark arrow, then, after approximately 20 yards, turn left and follow the public footpath sign and Harcamlow Way waymark arrow towards the church (St Peter and St Paul) at Fenstanton. Walk through the churchyard (past the church), then through a gate at the main entrance. Turn right onto Church Lane. Follow Church Lane to Chequer Street, then follow Chequer Street back to the pub.

PLACES OF INTEREST NEARBY

St Ives, off the A1096, a market town with a famous 15th-century bridge, is approximately 2 miles north of Fenstanton.

Swavesey
The White Horse Inn

MAP: OS EXPLORER 225 (GR 361689) | **WALK 16** | **DISTANCE:** 2¾ MILES

DIRECTIONS TO START: SWAVESEY IS APPROXIMATELY 1½ MILES NORTH OF THE A14, MIDWAY BETWEEN CAMBRIDGE AND HUNTINGDON. FOLLOW THE SIGNED SLIP ROAD (BY THE TRINITY FOOT PUBLIC HOUSE) OFF THE A14 TO THE VILLAGE. THE WHITE HORSE INN IS SITUATED AT THE NORTHERN END OF SWAVESEY'S MAIN STREET. **PARKING:** FREE CAR PARKING ON MARKET SQUARE IN FRONT OF THE WHITE HORSE INN.

This easy circuit takes the walker past a number of man-made lakes (the result of gravel extraction), along a short stretch of the River Great Ouse and over quiet countryside tracks. The lakes are a well landscaped home to wildfowl and are regularly used by anglers. Swavesey, a quiet village by the River Great Ouse, is home to around 2,000 people. It lies on the Greenwich Meridian, and is also home to the MG Owners' Club. Farming is still the main industry in Swavesey, but, due to mechanization, employs a fraction of the people it did in years gone by.

The White Horse Inn

This homely two-bar village pub dates from about 1620. The walls are decorated with hunting pictures, barrel taps and horse bits, and, unusually, there is also a well-stocked library. The White Horse Inn is open on Monday to Friday from 12 noon to 2.30 pm and from 6 pm to 11 pm. On Saturday it is open all day from 11.30 am to 11 pm and on Sunday from 12 noon to 10.30 pm. Beers are Flowers IPA, Boddingtons Bitter; Morland Old Speckled Hen and guest ales, invariably from a local brewery. A selection of bottled ales is also available.

There is a tasty and extensive food menu on offer on Monday to Saturday from 12 noon to 2.15 pm and from 7 pm to 10 pm. Food is served at lunchtime only on Sunday from 12 noon to 2.15 pm. Telephone: 01954 232470.

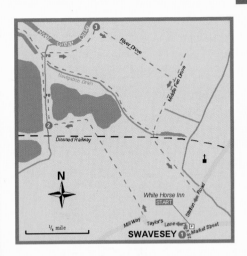

The Walk

① From the White Horse Inn turn right and follow the High Street to Taylor's Lane. Turn left and follow Taylor's Lane to the junction with Mill Way. Turn right at the junction, leave the metalled road and continue along the gravel track for about ³/₄ mile.

The disused railway track crossed on the route

The River Great Ouse

② Turn right, cross over the wooden stile and follow the yellow waymark arrow along the easterly bank of the drainage channel towards a footbridge. Cross over the foot-bridge, following the yellow waymark arrow, and continue in the same direction, following the westerly bank of the drainage channel towards a single lock gate. Turn right just before the lock gate, cross over it and follow the raised grass track along the course of the River Great Ouse.

③ Turn right and follow River Drove (a dirt track) to Middle Fen Drove. Turn right and follow Middle Fen Drove (a gravel track) back to Station Road. Turn right and follow Station Road back to the White Horse Inn.

> **PLACES OF INTEREST NEARBY**
>
> **Pike and Eel Hotel**, at the end of Overcote Lane, Needingworth, off the A1123 east of St Ives, is a 17th-century, oak-beamed listed building. It is located by a marina where a ferry used to cross the River Great Ouse from Over, just north of Swavesey. It has a large restaurant and riverside views and is open on Monday to Saturday from 11 am to 11 pm and on Sunday from 12 noon to 10.30 pm. Telephone: 01480 463336.

Stretham
The Lazy Otter

DIRECTIONS TO START: THE LAZY OTTER IS SITUATED ON A MINOR ROAD JUST OFF THE A10, APPROXIMATELY 2 MILES SOUTH OF STRETHAM AND 6 MILES SOUTH OF ELY. THE TURN-OFFS FROM THE A10 TO THE PUB ARE BOTH SIGNPOSTED. **PARKING:** IN THE PUB CAR PARK.

The walk from the Lazy Otter is a short, simple, easy leg-stretch along a quiet section of the River Great Ouse. The closest village is Stretham, some 2 miles to the north. The Stretham Old Engine (a large beam pumping engine dating from the 19th century) is a part of the Fens' industrial heritage, and is housed in a brick-built pumping station close to the furthest extent of the walk. Standing proudly at the end of the High Street is Tower Windmill, another reminder of Stretham's past.

The Lazy Otter

Pleasantly set alongside the River Great Ouse between Ely and Cambridge, the Lazy Otter has a riverside beer garden and a marina, which houses around forty narrow boats. It is open on Monday to Saturday from 11 am to 11 pm and from 12 noon to 10.30 pm on Sunday. The beers are Marston's Pedigree, Wadworth 6X, Nethergate Suffolk Best Bitter and Courage Best Bitter. A selection of bottled ales is also available.

Food is served on Monday to Thursday from 12 noon to 2.30 pm and from 6 pm to 9 pm; on Friday from 12 noon to 2.30 pm and 6 pm to 10 pm; on Saturday from 12 noon to 3 pm and 6 pm to 10 pm; on Sunday from 12 noon to 6 pm. The restaurant has a good selection of well-prepared meals, and a fine view of the river and the marina. Bar snacks and a vegetarian option are also available. Telephone: 01353 649780.

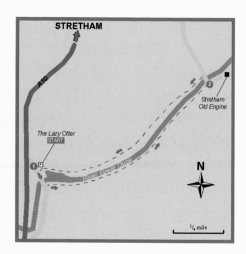

The Walk

① Turn left from the Lazy Otter and follow the metalled road over a bridge. Roughly 20 yards beyond the bridge there is a public footpath sign. Turn left and follow this sign through a kissing-gate and along the raised riverside path for approximately 1 mile.

Looking back towards the Lazy Otter and the marina

The Stretham Old Engine

② Turn left and cross over the bridge. Turn immediately left at the public footpath sign on the other side of the bridge. Follow this sign through a kissing-gate and along another raised riverside path all the way back to the Lazy Otter. NB: The raised path is set back from the riverside by about 20 yards.

PLACES OF INTEREST NEARBY

The **Stretham Old Engine**, which can be found by the riverside approximately 200 yards from the bridge at the furthest extent of the walk, is an example of a land drainage steam engine dating from 1831. The engine and pumping station in which it is housed is scheduled as an Ancient Monument. It is usually open to the public from 1.30 pm to 5 pm on the second Sunday of each month and during bank holidays. For precise opening times and further information, including admission charges, contact the Stretham Engine Trust direct, telephone: 01353 649210.

Soham
The Cherry Tree

MAP: OS EXPLORER 226 (GR 603721) | **WALK 18** | DISTANCE: 2½ MILES

DIRECTIONS TO START: FOLLOW THE A1123 TO THE ROUNDABOUT JUNCTION WITH THE A142; OR VICE VERSA. AT THE ROUNDABOUT TAKE THE EXIT BETWEEN THE A1123 AND THE A142; THIS IS FORDHAM ROAD. FOLLOW FORDHAM ROAD TO THE CHERRY TREE. **PARKING:** IN THE PUB CAR PARK.

Soham is situated in flat, fenland countryside, midway between Ely and Newmarket. Now a busy market town, it has been settled for at least 4,000 years and plenty of evidence has been found to show that both the Romans and the Anglo Saxons were settled here. The present church dates back to the 12th century and boasts a fine hammerbeam roof.

Our stroll is a leisurely affair, taking the walker through part of this thriving town and along well-defined paths to sample the wide open skyscape that is such a feature of this part of Cambridgeshire.

The Cherry Tree

The interior of this modern looking brick-built pub is in two parts: the bar area and the dining area. Both are comfortable and pleasant, and they are becomingly divided by wooden trellising. There is a large beer garden within which there is a bandstand, used by visiting brass bands for concerts on summer evenings, usually Sundays. These are usually well attended and accompanied by a barbecue.

The pub is open on Monday to Friday from 11 am to 3 pm and 6 pm to 11 pm; on Saturday it is open all day from 11 am to 11 pm (subject to trade); on Sunday the hours are 12 noon to 3 pm and 7 pm to 10.30 pm. The beers are Greene King Abbot Ale, IPA, Brewer's Bitter and XS. A selection of bottled ales is also available. Food is served all week from 12 noon to 2 pm and from 7 pm to 9.30 pm. Telephone: 01353 720405.

The Walk

① Just outside the Cherry Tree there is a crossroads. Cross over the main road here and follow Regal Lane to a left-hand bend. Bear left around the bend and continue on, following the road (now Brook Street) a further 30 yards or so to the junction with Greenhills. Turn right and follow Greenhills roughly 50 yards to another junction. Bear right at this junction and continue on along the road. At both junctions there are Soham Millennium Walk signs which can also be followed. Take care here, Greenhills is a Y-shaped road, and turning right from Brook Street after 30 yards or so or second right after about 50 yards will both lead to Greenhills. At the

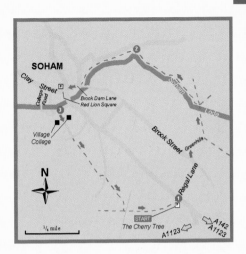

end of the metalled road (Greenhills) there is a forked junction. Do not turn right here, instead, bear left and continue on along a gravel/dirt track, following another Soham Millennium Walk sign. The track leads to farm outbuildings, and just before it reaches them there is a junction. Bear right at this junction, away from the outbuildings, and continue on along a grass/dirt track that runs between two hedgerows to a

PLACES OF INTEREST NEARBY

Wicken Fen is a national nature reserve, signposted off the A1123 just to the south of Wicken village: 3 miles south-west of Soham, 9 miles south of Ely, and 17 miles north-east of Cambridge (via the A10). This is the oldest nature reserve in the county, 100 years young in 1999. It is strikingly rich in plant, insect and bird life, and preserves a unique fragment of the wilderness that once covered much of East Anglia. There is a Visitors' Centre, open Tuesday to Saturday, 10 am to 5 pm, all year round except 25th December and occasionally during the winter; telephone 01353 720274. The fen is open all year round from dawn to dusk except for 25th December. Some paths may be closed in very wet weather.

A footbridge over the Soham Lode

located on Red Lion Square, along which the walk continues. Red Lion Square soon becomes Clay Street. Follow Clay Street to a double roundabout by Soham library. Do not turn left here, but instead continue straight on to the junction with College Road. Turn left and follow College Road to a bridge over the river (Soham Lodge again). Cross over the bridge and follow the road as it bears sharply left.

③ Turn right at the junction and follow both the public footpath and Soham Millennium Walk signs along a broad concrete path which passes through the grounds of the Village College to a small car park. Pass through the car park, cross over the road, and then follow the Soham Millennium Walk sign along a metalled footpath to a dirt/grass track; the distance between the second small zebra crossing to the track is only about 10 yards). Follow the dirt/grass track straight on, in the same direction as before; it initially passes to the left of a brick outbuilding, then continues on between two hedgerows. After about 100 yards there is a concrete/metal stile. Cross over this stile, following the Soham Millennium Walk waymark arrow to continue along the track as it runs between a hedgerow and, initially, a wooden fence line. The dirt/grass track eventually leads to a gravel/dirt track. Bear left at this point and follow the gravel/dirt track the 20 or so yards to a metalled road. Cross directly over the metalled road and continue on along a vehicle-rutted, grassy gravel/dirt track, following the Soham Millennium Walk and public byway signs. The track eventually leads to a junction. Turn left at the junction and follow the Soham Millennium Walk sign along another track which should be followed all the way back to the Cherry Tree.

concrete footbridge. Cross over the footbridge, then turn immediately left and follow the grass track along the riverside (Soham Lode) for just under $1/2$ mile.

② Where the riverside is fenced-off, the grass track continues straight on (jinking slightly to the right, a little away from the riverside), past the back of residential accommodation, to a bend in a metalled road. By the bend, the grass track joins up with a metalled footpath. Bear slightly left and continue on along the metalled footpath, as it runs past the back of more houses, eventually emerging at another bend in another metalled road (Brook Dam Lane). Do not turn right at the bend, but instead continue on along Brook Dam Lane, in roughly the same direction as before, to a T-junction. If possible, take a little time out at the junction in order to visit the excellent Red Lion public house. This is next to the war memorial which is

Saxon Street
The Reindeer

MAP: OS EXPLORER 210 (GR 679593) | **WALK 19** | **DISTANCE:** 2¾ MILES

DIRECTIONS TO START: FOLLOW THE A1304 INTO NEWMARKET TO THE JUNCTION WITH THE B1063, THEN TAKE THE B1063 SOUTH-EAST TO THE JUNCTION WITH THE B1103. SAXON STREET IS SIGNPOSTED FROM THIS JUNCTION. **PARKING:** IN THE PUB CAR PARK.

'The Street,' as it is known locally, is a well kept village with many lovingly restored and improved old properties. It has a very close association with nearby Newmarket and boasts several modern buildings devoted to the care of racehorses. In fact, if you like horses, this is definitely the walk for you, passing, as it does, several well-kept stud farms. In fact the whole area has a decidedly equine feel to it, which, being so close to Newmarket, is of course no big surprise. It doesn't matter how much the locals think they're in Suffolk, however, it's still in Cambridgeshire.

The Reindeer

There is a large bar area with a wood-beamed ceiling and tiled floor in this comfortable pub. The landlord believes in fresh vegetables and home cooking and keeps the ale in good condition. There is also a large beer garden for the summer months.

Although closed all day on Monday, the Reindeer is open on Tuesday to Saturday from 12 noon to 2.30 pm and from 6 pm to 11 pm. On Sunday it is open from 12 noon to 3 pm and 6 pm to 10.30 pm. The beers are Adnams Bitter and Broadside. Some bottled ales are also available. There is a dining area in the bar, but the separate restaurant area, with its varnished floorboards and stylish decorations, is a must see. Weekend lunchtimes can be very busy, and booking in advance is recommended. Food is served on Tuesday to Saturday from 12 noon to 2 pm and from 6.30 pm to 10 pm; on Sunday from 12 noon to 2.30 pm and from 6.30 pm to 9 pm. Telephone: 01638 730989.

The Walk

① Turn left from the Reindeer and follow the main road (The Street). Roughly 40 yards beyond the T-junction with School Road, on the right-hand side of The Street, there is a gap in a hedgerow. The gap is quite discreet and is next to the road sign warning of a left-hand bend in the road. It is marked by a largely obscured public footpath sign. Follow this sign through the gap and along the narrow dirt track. The track runs approximately 10 yards through a thicket and out onto a junction with a grass track which is bounded on one side by a

hedgerow, and on the other by a wooden fence. Turn right at this junction and follow the grass track, keeping the hedgerow to the immediate right-hand side and the wooden fence to the immediate left-hand side. The track quickly leads to a set of two wooden slat gates which fence off a strip of land that joins two otherwise separate fields. Pass through the two gates and continue on along the grass track, in the same direction as before, to a junction with a single track metalled road. Turn left at this junction and continue along the road for about 400 yards.

② Leave the road at the outbuildings (sharp left-hand bend), and continue straight on the 15 or so yards to a wooden gate. Pass through the wooden gate, turn right and follow the grass track, as it runs between two hedgerows, for roughly 1/3 mile to a main road. Turn right and follow the main road the 100 yards or so to the Red Lion public house in Cheveley. After a satisfying visit (optional!) to the Red Lion, continue following the main road (Little Green, which eventually, and unnoticeably, becomes Oak Lane) all the way to a

A familiar sight around Newmarket

T-junction (just over ¹/₂ mile). At the T-junction, cross directly over the road to a wooden gate. Pass through the gate and follow the public footpath sign to bear slightly left and continue along a relatively broad grass track, keeping a hedgerow to the left-hand side and a fence line to the right-hand side (ie don't bear/turn right).

③ At the corner of the field, pass through a gap in the hedgerow, then follow a yellow waymark arrow right. Continue on along a similarly broad grass track as before that runs between two hedgerows; do not turn left once through the gap, and do not continue straight on the 5 yards or so that leads through another gap in another hedgerow. After about 200 yards there is a junction. Continue straight on along the grass track in the same direction as before at this junction, ie do not turn right. Follow the track as it eventually bears right, past a small copse of trees, and on to a three-way power pole by two hedgerow gaps. Bear left at the pole, passing through the gap to the left, then bear right and follow the grass track in the same direction as before; only this time the track runs between a hedgerow to the right-hand side and the back of residential accommodation to the left-hand side. After about 150 yards the track comes to a junction with Cheveley Road. Turn left and follow Cheveley Road to the junction with The Street, then turn right and follow The Street back to the Reindeer.

PLACES OF INTEREST NEARBY

Newmarket. A walk round the town reveals many attractions, including the National Horse-Racing Museum (a must) the Clock Tower (1887), High Street; King Edward VII Memorial Hall and Gardens (1914), opposite the Jockey Club; Nell Gwynne's House, Palace Street; Real Tennis Court, Fitzroy Street. For further information, contact the Newmarket Tourist Information Centre, telephone 01638 667200.

Kirtling Green
The Red Lion

MAP: OS EXPLORER 210 (GR 683559)   **WALK 20**   DISTANCE: 2½ MILES

DIRECTIONS TO START: TAKE THE B1063 FROM NEWMARKET AND FOLLOW THE SIGNS TO SAXON STREET AND THEN TO KIRTLING. CARRY ON THE ROAD THROUGH KIRTLING ON TO KIRTLING GREEN. **PARKING:** IN THE PUB CAR PARK.

The walk encompasses green paths that pass over a gently rolling terrain. Much of the route also skirts most of Lucy Wood. Kirtling Green lies in an area of undulating hillsides and valleys, farmland and pastures, all frequently interspersed with woods and copses of various sizes and tree types.

The Red Lion

This friendly locals' pub has a tiled floor, an open fire/stove and a wood-panelled bar. Some of the remarkable decorations are a bit on the martial side; watch out for the mace and chain. Thankfully, however, they are the antitheses of the relaxed atmosphere.

The Red Lion is closed all day on Monday but is open on Tuesday to Saturday from 11 am to 2 pm and 7 pm to 11 pm; on Sunday from 12 noon to 3 pm and 7 pm to 10.30 pm. The beers are Adnams Bitter and Fisherman. Some bottled ales are also available. There is a separate dining area and food is served on Tuesday to Saturday from 12 noon to 2 pm and from 7 pm to 9.30 pm; on Sunday from 12 noon to 2.30 pm and 7 pm to 9 pm. Telephone: 01638 731976.

The Walk

① From the Red Lion turn right and follow The Street to the junction with Malting End and The Green. Turn right and follow The Green for about ⅓ mile.

② Turn right at the public footpath sign and continue on along a vehicle-rutted gravel track to Stone Cottage; do not follow the public byway sign positioned just a few yards before the public footpath sign. Just beyond the entrance to Stone Cottage there is a wooden fence. Pass through this fence and continue on in the same direction as before. From the fence the footpath consists of a grass track that runs between two tree lines/hedgerows. The grass track ends at a clearing, after roughly 200 yards. Turn right at the clearing and follow the dirt/grass track along the edge of the field

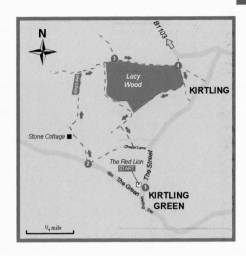

towards King's Belt Wood, and eventually down to a corner of the field at the far edge of the woodland. At the corner of the field (by a gap in the hedgerow and the junction with another dirt/grass track) bear sharp right and continue on towards Lucy Wood, keeping the hedgerow to the left-hand side. Approximately 50 yards from Lucy Wood, turn left and pass through a gap in the hedgerow. Once through the gap turn immediately right and continue along a dirt/gravel track, keeping the hedgerow to the right-hand side.

③ Pass through a gap in the hedgerow at the corner of the field, then turn right at the junction and follow the dirt/gravel track along the edge of Lucy Wood for about ⅓ mile.

④ At the junction by the sharp left-hand bend, turn right, pass through a metal kissing-gate and continue on, up a gentle slope, along the right-hand edge of the field, keeping Lucy Wood to the immediate right-hand side. At the corner of Lucy Wood, at the top of the slope, bear sharp

Lucy Wood

right and continue along the edge of the field, some 50 yards or thereabouts, to a wooden stile. Cross over the stile and follow the grass track that runs between a fence line and the edge of Lucy Wood. After about 400 yards the track is diverted slightly onto a dirt track that runs parallel with the fence line, in the same direction as before, but roughly 2 yards into the woods: the point where this happens is marked with a yellow waymark arrow. The dirt track emerges from Lucy Wood onto a junction with a grass track, marked by a waymarker post. Turn left at the post and continue along a grass track, keeping the hedgerow and a small ditch to the left-hand side. After about 150 yards turn left and cross over a wooden footbridge. Once over the footbridge continue along a grass track that runs between two fence lines. After about 200 yards there is a junction,

continue straight on at this point; the grass track now runs between a fence line and a hedge at the back of a private residence. Turn left approximately 50 yards further on, at the junction with the single-track metalled road (Chapel Lane). Follow Chapel Lane for about 250 yards to the main road (The Street). Turn right and follow The Street back to the Red Lion.

> ### PLACES OF INTEREST NEARBY
> **Sascombe Vineyards**, The Thrift, Bradley Road, Kirtling Green, Cambridgeshire, CB8 9JB. Follow Malting End east, it soon becomes Bradley Road. After about ½ mile, take the second right turn onto The Thrift. Follow The Thrift approximately ½ mile to the entrance of the vineyard. The 12 acre Sascombe Vineyards is open to the public all year round. Telephone 01440 783100 for opening times and further information on the vineyard's products and English wines in general.

Fen Ditton
The Ancient Shepherds

MAP: OS EXPLORER 209 (GR 485602) | **WALK 21** | **DISTANCE:** 4¾ MILES

DIRECTIONS TO START: TURN OFF THE A14 AT THE JUNCTION WITH THE B1047, THEN HEAD SOUTH TO FEN DITTON. THE ANCIENT SHEPHERDS IS LOCATED JUST OFF THE B1047 ON THE HIGH STREET. **PARKING:** IN THE PUB CAR PARK.

The walk essentially follows an approximately 2 mile stretch of the River Cam into Cambridge, via Baits Bite Lock (just to the north of Fen Ditton). This stretch of the Cam is gently active, and it would be a surprise to walk it at any time of the year and not see at least a couple of boat crews rowing up and down. It's not so busy that it puts off the wildlife, however, and there are usually swans on the river. Fen Ditton started out life as a defensive dyke created by the Iceni tribe to protect themselves from Roman invaders attacking from the south; it didn't work. These days Fen Ditton is a modestly large and very pleasant village.

The Ancient Shepherds

Originally built as three cottages in 1540, the Ancient Shepherds is now a listed building. The pub oozes atmosphere, and the lounge, with its leather Chesterfields and low tables, is particularly inviting. The beer garden is nice and shady on a hot day.

The opening hours on Monday to Saturday are from 12 noon to 2.30 pm and from 6.30 pm to 11 pm; Sunday from 12 noon to 3.30 pm only. Flowers IPA is always on offer, together with guest ales. Bottled beers are also available. The menu is sumptuous and caters for a wide range of tastes and there are usually seasonal specialities to be found. All dishes are served with crisp and tasty vegetables with not an oven chip in sight. Food times are: Monday 12 noon to 2.15 pm only; Tuesday to Saturday 12 noon to 2.15 pm and 6.30 pm to 9.30 pm; Sunday from 12 noon to 3.15 pm. Telephone: 01223 293280.

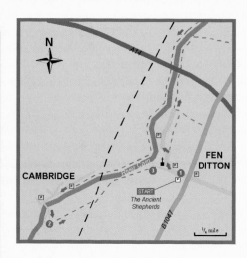

The Walk

① From the pub turn left and follow the High Street to the war memorial by the King's Head public house. Turn right at the war memorial and follow Church Street, which becomes Green End at a left-hand bend in the road. Continue to follow Green End, round a right-hand bend, past/via the Plough public house, to the junction at the end of the metalled road. At the junction follow the public footpath/Fen Rivers Way sign straight on to a kissing-gate, then pass through the kissing-gate and follow the public footpath sign along a grass/dirt track to Baits Bite Lock. The track runs roughly parallel with the River Cam and passes

through several kissing-gates, under a bridge (a fly-over section of the A14) and lastly through a riverside copse of trees (the copse can become very overgrown during the warmer months, so think twice about wearing shorts). If all else fails, just follow the route of the Cam and/or the Fens Rivers Way waymark arrows to the lock. At Baits Bite Lock cross over the two footbridges, then once on the opposite bank of the river turn immediately left and follow the dirt track along the riverside for about 1³/₄ miles to the Pike and Eel public house. From the pub turn left and follow Water Street to the Green Dragon public house. Cross over the footbridge directly opposite the Green Dragon and carry straight on to a junction between two metalled footpaths. Turn left at this junction and continue on.

② Turn left and follow the straight dirt track to a railway footbridge. Cross over this footbridge and continue on, almost immediately crossing over a further, small footbridge. On the other side of the small footbridge, follow the grass track to the left; heading in the direction of the two

Baits Bite Lock

houses in the middle distance on the opposite bank of the Cam (one white house, one pink house at time of writing). The grass track leads to a wooden footbridge. Cross over this footbridge and follow the grass track, as it runs parallel with the route of the Cam, towards Fen Ditton.

③ Pass through the kissing-gate and follow the dirt track round to the left, for approximately 20 yards, to a junction. At the junction bear right and follow the dirt track (which soon becomes metalled) onto the High Street, then follow the High Street back to the Ancient Shepherds.

PLACES OF INTEREST NEARBY

Milton Country Park, signposted from, and close to, the A10/A14 junction just north-west of Fen Ditton, is a mix of woods, grass and water. It is also home to the Sensory Garden, an area which boasts a wide variety of plants chosen for their texture and aroma. There is a visitors' centre and a car park. Telephone: 01223 420060.

Hardwick
The Blue Lion

DIRECTIONS TO START: HARDWICK IS SITUATED ON THE A428, ROUGHLY 5 MILES WEST OF CAMBRIDGE; THE A428 CAN BE REACHED FROM THE M11/A14. IN THE CENTRE OF HARDWICK TURN SOUTHWARDS OFF THE A428 AND FOLLOW MAIN STREET TO THE BLUE LION. **PARKING:** IN THE PUB CAR PARK.

The first mention of Hardwick in the history books dates from AD 970 when a Benedictine monastery was established here. Alas, it is no more but the village still has a tranquil feel to it. The rural setting makes it hard to imagine that the city of Cambridge is so close.

This gentle stroll takes you along undulating footpaths and bridleways to sample some of the delights of this expanding village, surrounded as it is by farmland, orchards and woods.

The Blue Lion

This photogenic hostelry has a split-level bar and a bit of a split-level personality. The older part of the building is a mixture of brickwork, tiles, wooden beams and plaster; the newer part, mainly the dining room and especially the conservatory, looks much more modern. Throw in lots of horse brasses and framed pictures, stir in a couple of fireplaces, one with a large hearth, and it all sounds like a bit of a mishmash. Not so, however, for the Blue Lion is a tasteful looking pub with a convivial atmosphere. Besides, they have nice cats!

The opening hours are the same throughout the week, from 12 noon to 3 pm and from 5.30 pm to 11 pm. Greene King Abbot Ale and IPA are the beers available, as well as some bottled ales. The food is very tasty and there is a separate dining area. Meals are served on Monday to Friday from 12 noon to 2 pm and from 6.45 pm to 9 pm. Saturday and Sunday food times are flexible – booking advisable – from 12 noon. Telephone: 01954 210328.

The Walk

① Cross over the road and follow the public footpath sign immediately opposite the Blue Lion; the sign points to Comberton (1½) and Coton (2). The grass track passes between the houses and leads straight across a field to a copse of trees. Continue straight on along the grass track through the copse (approximately 30 yards), and keep following the pathway to a small wooded area. At the woods there is a wooden stile, climb over it and follow the grass track (and yellow waymark arrow) through the trees. Approximately 30 yards later, cross over a small wooden footbridge where the track emerges from the woods. At the junction on the other side of the footbridge continue straight on, following the yellow waymark arrow (Cambridge Green Belt Project) and keeping the hedgerow to the left-hand side. At the corner of the hedgerow turn left, following the yellow waymark arrow and the grass track; again keeping the hedgerow to the left-hand side. After about 300 yards there is a gap in the hedgerow, follow the yellow waymark arrow through the gap and continue along the grass track in the same direction as before, this time keeping the hedgerow to the right-hand side. At the corner of the field pass through another gap in the hedgerow, then follow the yellow waymark arrow and the grass track straight ahead. The track soon follows the course of Bin Brook past Common Farm and on to Long Road.

② Climb over the wooden stile, turn right and follow Long Road for approximately 100 yards. Turn right at the wooden public

The view towards Common Farm

bridleway sign marking the Wimpole Way. Follow this sign along the straight, grassy bridleway for about ½ mile, up the hill to the wooded area (Starve Goose Plantation). At the top of the hill there is a junction and a wooden footbridge. Do not cross over the footbridge; instead, turn left, following the white waymark arrow, and continue along the bridleway (in between two hedgerows) for about 200 yards to a junction by some wooden fence posts. Turn sharp right at the fence posts and continue along the bridleway for about 1 mile, back towards Hardwick. Turn right at Main Street and follow the road back to the Blue Lion.

PLACES OF INTEREST NEARBY

Madingley Hall is off the junction of the A428/A1303, roughly 2 miles north-east of Hardwick and 3½ miles west of Cambridge. Built in 1543, and owned by the University of Cambridge since 1948, it is used today partly as student accommodation and partly as a location for continuing education courses. The Hall itself is not open to the public, but visitors are welcome to walk around the gardens and grounds and to visit the parish church of St Mary Magdalene (just inside the main gate). Another delight of Madingley is the picturesque old thatched inn, the **Three Horseshoes**, with its cosy bar, conservatory dining room, and garden extending all the way to the local cricket pitch.

Eaton Socon
The Rivermill Tavern

MAP: OS EXPLORER 208 (GR 173587)   **WALK 23**   DISTANCE: 3 MILES

DIRECTIONS TO START: TURN OFF THE A1 AT THE JUNCTION WITH THE A428, JUST SOUTH OF ST NEOTS. ALMOST IMMEDIATELY AFTER DOING THIS THERE IS A ROUNDABOUT. TAKE THE B1428 EXIT AND CONTINUE FOR ABOUT ½ MILE TO THE JUNCTION WITH SCHOOL LANE. TURN RIGHT AND FOLLOW SCHOOL LANE TO THE RIVERMILL TAVERN. **PARKING:** IN THE PUB CAR PARK.

A walk along the River Great Ouse, a chance to visit and explore St Neots and more good pubs on the route (see map) than you can shake an average sized stick at! The marina by the Rivermill Tavern is quite charming and there is also a very nice tearoom and gallery next door to both (Emily's), which does a tempting cream tea. St Neots is the largest town in the administrative county of Cambridgeshire, but remains largely unspoiled and full of small architectural gems.

The Rivermill Tavern

The basic structure and theme of this former storehouse/mill is wood. It's in the beams of the walls, the ceiling and the balcony, and the whole place is quite atmospheric of times past. There is plenty of seating just outside the pub entrance by the marina. When the weather is good it is wonderfully relaxing to sit there and watch the boats go by; it feels leisurely just to remember it.

The Rivermill Tavern is open all day, every day from 12 noon to 11 pm (to 10.30 pm on Sunday). The beers are Greene King IPA and Abbot Ale, along with guests. A selection of bottled ales is also available. The food is good, standard pub fare, with a Mexican twist. It is served on Monday to Thursday from 12.30 pm to 2.30 pm and from 6.30 pm to 9.30 pm and on Friday to Sunday from 12 noon to 3 pm and 6.30 pm to 10 pm. Telephone: 01480 219612.

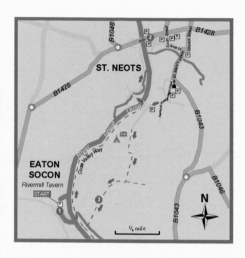

The Walk

① Bear left on leaving the Rivermill Tavern, head past the marina and continue on across the weir in order to reach the opposite bank of the river (River Great Ouse). Immediately on the other side of the river, turn left and follow the riverside grass track for about ³/₄ mile towards the centre of St Neots. The grass track ends at a small car park. Pass through the car park, following the yellow Ouse Valley Way waymark arrows. After about 30 yards the arrows lead round to the left and across a large, arched wooden footbridge, spanning the river. Once across the footbridge there is a fork in the metalled footpaths. Take the right-hand fork and follow the footpath for about 50 yards to another arched wooden footbridge. Cross over this footbridge, and immediately on the other side there is a crossroads between two metalled footpaths. Turn right at the crossroads and follow the riverside footpath north. After passing under a raised road section and up a staircase, the footpath eventually joins up with the B1428. Follow the B1428 over the river to the Bridge House public house. NB: The yellow Ouse Valley Way waymark arrows can be followed from immediately after the point of crossing over the weir, near the start of the walk, all the way to the Bridge House.

② From the Bridge House turn left and follow the main road, past/via the Old Falcon Hotel and the Golden Ball public houses, to the junction with South Street. Turn right and follow South Street, bearing sharp left around a bend (where the road becomes Brook Street). Take the next right turn and follow St Mary's Street (B1043) to a junction by St Mary the Virgin church. Turn right at this junction and follow Montagu Street to Hardwick Road. Turn right and follow Hardwick Road for about

One of the many fine pubs passed on the walk

50 yards, then turn right again, following the camping and caravan sign along a road past the Coneygeare public house and on towards a playground. There are two public footpath signs by the playground. Follow the sign that bears left (ie not the one that leads across the wooden footbridge) and continue on along the road to the camping and caravan site. To the immediate left of the camping and caravan site there is a grass track. Follow this track as it runs between a hedgerow and a fence. Follow the track to a gap in the far corner of the hedgerow. Pass through the gap, into an open field, and immediately on the other side turn left and follow the grass track the 30 or so yards to a concrete post next to a wooden power pole: two grass tracks converge at a crossroads near the concrete post. Turn right at the crossroads and continue on along the grass/dirt track which runs alongside, and to the immediate right of, the concrete fencing posts, and parallel with the overhead power lines. The track leads to a T-junction with a gravel track. Turn right at this junction and follow the gravel track in the general direction of the River Great Ouse.

③ Do not turn left onto the dirt track. Instead, keep going in the same direction along the gravel track for another 250 yards or so, then turn right and cross over a concrete footbridge. Immediately on the other side of the footbridge turn right and follow the dirt track through the trees to the weir. Turn left and cross over the weir to return to the Rivermill Tavern.

PLACES OF INTEREST NEARBY

St Neots Museum, New Street, St Neots is a repository of local history and is well worth a visit. It is open on Wednesday to Friday from 10.30 am to 4.30 pm. Telephone: 01480 388788 (St Neots Tourist Information Centre can also be contacted on this number).

Abbotsley
The Eight Bells of Abbotsley

MAP: OS EXPLORER 208 (GR 229565)   **WALK 24**   **DISTANCE:** 4½ MILES

DIRECTIONS TO START: TURN OFF THE A1 AT THE JUNCTION WITH THE A428, JUST SOUTH OF ST NEOTS. FOLLOW THE A428 FOR ABOUT 1¼ MILES TO THE JUNCTION WITH THE B1046, THEN FOLLOW THE B1046 SOUTH TO ABBOTSLEY VILLAGE. **PARKING:** IN THE PUB CAR PARK.

Abbotsley is a delightful, small village with a population of about 500. It is just four miles east of St Neots and boasts its own duck pond and a fine church, said to be early 14th century. Standing on high ground, the church dedicated to St Margaret of Antioch is well worth a visit.

The walk from the Eight Bells of Abbotsley past St Margaret's church, provides a pleasant stroll in the countryside, along quiet farm tracks and lanes; nothing hugely spectacular, but tranquil and refreshing at all times of the year.

The Eight Bells of Abbotsley

Summertime sees a great splash of colour growing from the hanging basket by the main entrance of this welcoming and friendly local. Inside, the decor consists mainly of trophies, tankards, plates and horse brasses. The Eight Bells is open on Monday to Friday from 12 noon to 2 pm and from 5.30 pm to 11 pm, all day from 12 noon to 11 pm on Saturday and 12 noon to 10.30 pm on Sunday. The beers are Greene King IPA and Abbot Ale, together with guests and bottled ales.

There is a cosy dining room where a large menu is on offer, and snacks can be obtained at the bar. Food is served on Monday to Saturday from 12 noon to 2 pm and from 7 pm to 9 pm, and at lunchtime only on Sunday from 12 noon to 2 pm. Telephone: 01767 677305.

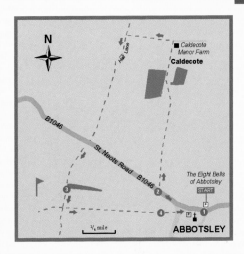

The Walk

① From the pub turn right and follow the High Street as it eventually becomes St Neots Road for about ¹/₂ mile. It takes you past St Margaret's church and the Jolly Abbot public house.

② Turn right and follow the public footpath sign to Hail Lane along a single-track concrete roadway. Follow this roadway for about 1³/₄ miles all the way to Caldecote Manor Farm, Caldecote. The very end of this stretch of the walk leads through Caldecote Manor Farm farmyard to a small T-junction. Turn left at the T-junction and follow the dirt track, keeping the hedgerow to the left-hand side. The dirt track leads to the corner of a field and a wooden waymarker post. Follow the yellow waymark arrow on this post that points to the left, and continue on along Hail Lane (a fairly well-rutted bridleway), keeping the hedgerow to the right-hand side. Follow Hail Lane for approximately 1 mile to St Neots Road. Cross directly over St Neots Road (B1046) and follow the public bridleway sign straight ahead along the dirt track, keeping the hedgerow to the right-hand side.

③ At a loosely defined crossroads continue straight on along the dirt track, with the hedgerow still on the right-hand side. The dirt track leads to a small copse of trees in the corner of the field. Do not follow the dirt track into the trees, but instead bear left and follow the edge of the copse for about 30 yards to a grass track. Follow the grass track more or less in a straight line due east for about 1¹/₄ miles all the way back to Abbotsley. For the first ¹/₂ mile a hedgerow runs to the immediate right of the grass track. The grass track runs parallel with overhead power lines all the way back to Abbotsley, and the route is also marked by yellow waymark arrows.

Abbotsley

④ Cross over the wooden stile and follow the yellow waymark arrow straight on along the grass track in the direction of St Margaret's church. After approximately 20 yards cross over another wooden stile and again follow a yellow waymark arrow straight on (still in the direction of St Margaret's), across a playing field to a metalled road. Follow the metalled road (Hardwick Lane) up the hill towards St Margaret's. At the road junction at the end of Hardwick Lane turn right, and after approximately 10 yards turn left at another road junction. Follow this road (High Green) past the Jolly Abbot public house to the High Street. Turn right and follow the High Street back to the Eight Bells of Abbotsley.

> **PLACES OF INTEREST NEARBY**
> **Wyboston Lakes Golf Club**, off the A1 just south of St Neots is an 18-hole public course with driving range. Telephone: 01480 223004.

Grantchester
The Red Lion

MAP: OS EXPLORER 209 (GR 434556)	**WALK 25**	DISTANCE: 5 MILES

DIRECTIONS TO START: TURN OFF THE M11 AT JUNCTION 12 AND FOLLOW THE SIGNS TO CAMBRIDGE. FROM THE FIRST ROUNDABOUT TAKE COTON ROAD ALL THE WAY INTO GRANTCHESTER. AT THE GREEN MAN PUBLIC HOUSE TURN LEFT AND FOLLOW THE ROAD TO THE RED LION. **PARKING:** IN THE PUB CAR PARK.

The walk starts off from Grantchester, passes through Grantchester Meadows and follows the old canal into the centre of Cambridge, where there is an option to break away and discover the city. Grantchester Meadows is where an embryonic Pink Floyd spent time 'grooving in a cave with a pict'. Singer, guitarist and rock god Syd Barrett still lives in Cambridge. The city itself is a captivating and beautiful place with its magnificent courtyards, bridges, riverside 'Backs' and a wealth of architectural styles. If its great rival Oxford is a city of 'dreaming spires', then Cambridge might well be described as a city of aspiring dreams. Here you are then – some fascinating pubs, a beautiful city and a pleasant riverside stroll, all in one walk!

The Red Lion

From the outside this is one of the most aesthetically pleasing pubs in Cambridge. It has a comfortable interior, if, in places, a bit dark. It is quite modern looking, but with its wood-beamed ceilings and wood-panelled bars it isn't soulless. It is, however, a big pub, so there shouldn't be a problem being served, even when it's busy. In summer the walled beer garden is delightful; in winter a nice big open fire in the pub makes things very cosy.

The Red Lion is open all day throughout the week, from 11 am to 11 pm on Monday to Saturday and from 12 noon to 10.30 pm on Sunday. The beers on offer are Greene King IPA and Abbot Ale. Some bottled ales are also available, together with a good wine list. There is a large dining area and food – reliable pub fare – is served every day from 12 noon till closing time. Telephone: 01223 840121.

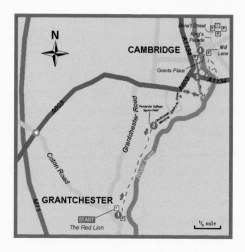

The Walk

① From the Red Lion turn left and follow the lane the 30 yards or so to a wooden kissing-gate. Pass through the kissing-gate and turn almost immediately left onto a metalled footpath. Follow this footpath (watching out for cyclists) for approximately 1¼ miles as it passes through Grantchester Meadows, alongside the gently meandering flow of the River Cam.

② Just beyond Pembroke College Sports Field the footpath widens out and soon joins up with a street called Grantchester Meadows. Keep going straight on along the street to a three-way fork in the road. Carry on along the middle fork (Eltisley Avenue) to the junction with Grantchester Street. Bear left at this junction and continue along Grantchester Street to the traffic lights. At the traffic lights there is a crossroads; turn right and follow the road for about ¼ mile to a metal footbridge, keeping a hedgerow and the recreation ground (Lammas Land) to the left-hand side. Cross over the metal footbridge, pass through a metal gate, then turn immediately left and follow the metalled footpath as it runs alongside the disused canal.

③ Cross over the main road (A1134) at the pelican crossing, then continue along the canalside footpath, in the same direction as before, to a wooden footbridge (approximately 150 yards). Continue straight on at the footbridge in order to visit the Granta public house, have a meal in one of the restaurants or hire a punt. Having done all/some/none of that, cross over the footbridge and continue on along the metalled footpath to the left; ie don't turn right immediately on the other side of the footbridge. After about 150 yards the footpath comes to a junction. Bear left at

The delightful river frontage of the Granta pub

this junction and follow the metalled footpath alongside the River Cam to a brick footbridge. Cross over the brick footbridge and take the opportunity to visit the Mill public house; there are also more punts for hire close by. After the Mill/punting, there is an option to visit the Tourist Information Centre and discover Cambridge. To do so, carry on along Mill Lane. *Alternatively, to continue the walk without visiting the city, simply skip to point 4.* Turn left at the crossroads at the end of Mill Lane and follow the road (Trumpington Street/King's Parade) past Ede & Ravenscroft to Bene't Street. Turn right and follow Bene't Street past/via the Eagle, the Bath House and the Red Cow public houses to the Tourist Information Centre. The choice is now between finding out all there is to know about Cambridge, or retracing the walk back to the Mill public house, from where it will resume.

④ From the Mill follow Granta Place to a metal gate. Pass through the metal gate and follow the narrow gravel track along the edge of the field towards the main road (A1134). Roughly 100 yards before the A1134 turn right, then cross over the small wooden footbridge and head towards a much larger metal footbidge (Crusoe Bridge) over the River Cam. Cross over Crusoe Bridge, and once on the other side continue on the 10 or so yards it takes to cross over a small wooden footbridge to a junction with a metalled footpath. Turn left at the junction and follow the footpath to the main road (A1134). Cross directly over the A1134 and continue on along another metalled footpath, in much the same direction as before. Follow this footpath alongside the river to a bridge over the Cam. At the bridge there is a junction. Turn right at this junction and follow the metalled footpath approximately 40 yards to the metal footbridge. From this bridge it's just a case of retracing the walk back to the Red Lion at Grantchester – the views are quite different this way round!

PLACES OF INTEREST NEARBY

The city of **Cambridge**. There is so very much to do and see in this city, that it would be a real shame to miss out. It's just a pity that a few hours' diversion from the walk provides nothing other than the chance to briefly skim the surface of the many delights and distractions on offer. A good place to start, however, would be the Tourist Information Centre, which can also advise you on the wide variety of accommodation available in and around Cambridge, if you would like a longer stay. Telephone: 01223 322640.

Burrough Green
The Bull

MAP: OS EXPLORER 210 (GR 638555) | **WALK 26** | **DISTANCE:** 2¼ MILES

DIRECTIONS TO START: FOLLOW THE A1304 TO THE SOUTH-WEST OUTSKIRTS OF NEWMARKET, THEN TURN OFF ONTO THE B1061 AND FOLLOW THIS ROAD SOUTH FOR ROUGHLY 4¾ MILES TO BURROUGH GREEN AND THE BULL. **PARKING:** IN THE PUB CAR PARK.

This walk over level paths is no good if you're training for a marathon, but excellent if you're looking for an easy stroll in the countryside. The Icknield Way runs through the village and in fact, this ancient trackway cuts straight across the large village green where, during the summer months, cricket is played. The parish church of St Augustine was restored in the 18th century and has an impressively large tower which houses no less than five bells.

The circuit also takes in nearby Brinkley.

THE BULL

This cosy pub is popular with local walking groups. The beer is well kept and the atmosphere is friendly. It is open all week from 12 noon to 3 pm and from 6 pm to 11 pm. The beers are Greene King IPA and Abbot Ale, together with guest ales and bottled beer. Hot food and sandwiches are available every day from 12 noon to 2 pm and from 6 pm to 9 pm. Telephone: 01638 507480.

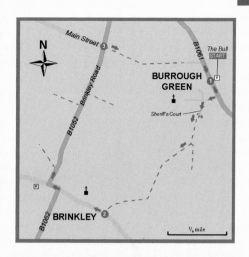

The Walk

① Turn left on leaving the Bull and follow the main road (Bradley Road) for about 100 yards to a crossroads. Turn right at the crossroads and follow the metalled road for another 100 yards or so. Turn left onto Sheriff's Court and continue on towards a metal gate. Immediately to the right of the metal gate there is a wooden footbridge. Cross over the footbridge and pass through a kissing-gate, then turn immediately left and continue on to the corner of the field, keeping the hedgerow to the left-hand side. The footbridge and the kissing-gate are both marked with yellow Icknield Way waymark arrows, which can also be followed. At the corner of the field, pass through a kissing-gate and cross over a wooden footbridge. On the other side of the footbridge, bear right and follow the grass track diagonally across the field towards a tree line/hedgerow (the grass track is quite broad, if not always greatly distinct, and is mildly vehicle-rutted); take care not to follow the track to the left which runs alongside a different tree line/hedgerow. The grass track meets the tree line/hedgerow at a wooden gate. Bear left just before the wooden gate and continue

to follow the grass track as it runs alongside the tree line/hedgerow in the direction of Brinkley. Eventually the grass track leads to a gap in the tree line/hedgerow, near the corner of the field. Turn right and pass through the gap, crossing over a wooden footbridge. Continue on across another field to a metal gate. Climb over the metal gate and continue straight ahead, passing a wooden outbuilding with a corrugated iron roof, and on to a wooden gate by the main road (High Street).

② Climb over the wooden gate, turn right and follow the High Street through Brinkley village to the junction with the B1052. At this junction continue straight ahead, along the B1052, for about 50 yards to another junction. At the second junction, if you want to visit Brinkley's Red Lion, continue straight ahead again (this time leaving the B1052) and follow the road the 100 or so yards to the pub. After the Red Lion, retrace the walk the 100 yards or so back to the junction with the B1052 and turn left. Walking along the footpath, follow the B1052 (Brinkley Road) northwards for approximately ⅔ mile.

The Icknield Way goes across the village green

③ Turn right at the crossroads between Brinkley Road, Main Street and the broad, grassy bridleway, follow the Icknield Way/Rider's Route sign (and any subsequent Icknield Way/Rider's Route signs) along the bridleway. The bridleway runs all the way back to the B1061 (Bradley Road) and the outskirts of Burrough Green, and a small metalled footpath runs along its left-hand edge. The last couple of hundred yards of the bridleway is almost fully metalled. At Bradley Road, turn right and continue on the last 250 yards or so back to the Bull.

PLACES OF INTEREST NEARBY

Newmarket Racecourses are off the junction of the A1303 and A1304, approximately 1½ miles to the south-west of Newmarket. General information, including the schedule of race meetings, is obtainable by telephone: 01638 675500. Guided tours of **The National Stud** are available between March and September, and during October race days. For further information telephone: 01638 666789. But if you do nothing else when in Newmarket, make sure you visit the **National Horse-Racing Museum** in the High Street; open all year. Telephone: 01638 667333.

Great Eversden
The Hoops

MAP: OS EXPLORER 209 (GR 364535) **WALK 27** **DISTANCE:** 2¾ MILES

DIRECTIONS TO START: FOLLOW THE M11 TO JUNCTION 12, THEN TURN OFF AND FOLLOW THE A603 WEST. ROUGHLY 3½ MILES FROM JUNCTION 12, TURN OFF THE A603 AND FOLLOW THE SIGNS FOR GREAT AND LITTLE EVERSDEN. THE HOOPS IS SITUATED APPROXIMATELY 1 MILE TO THE NORTH OF THE A603. **PARKING:** IN THE PUB CAR PARK.

Rolling hills, panoramic views and a stroll through the woods are the main features on offer. Much of the walk passes through open farmland, but part of it passes through Eversden Wood, a large area of mixed woodland. The picturesque Great Eversden and its twin village Little Eversden are situated to the south-west of Cambridge, between Wimpole Hall and the Mullard Observatory radio telescope. Both villages have been associated together since the time of the Domesday Book, but ironically, these days Little Eversden has a population nearly three times the size of Great.

The Hoops

This welcoming pub has some lovely wood features: beams, furniture and panelling. The stone floor helps keep visitors cool in the summer, and an open fire provides the heat in winter. The Hoops is open on Saturday from 12 noon to 3.30 pm and 7 pm to 11 pm and on Sunday from 11 am to 3.30 pm. It is closed all day on Monday and open in the evenings only from Tuesday to Friday between 7 pm and 11 pm.

The beer is Flowers IPA and some bottled ales are also available. Food is served at lunchtime on Saturday and Sunday. Telephone for details: 01223 264008.

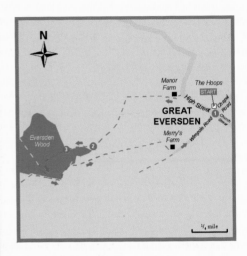

The Walk

① The Hoops is situated at a crossroads between Church Street, High Street, Chapel Road and Wimpole Road. Facing the crossroads from Chapel Road, turn right and follow Church Street (which almost immediately becomes High Street). Continue along the road, through Great Eversden, for about ⅓ mile to a sharp right-hand bend. At the bend turn left and follow the larger of the two public footpath signs over a metal gate and along a moderately vehicle-rutted, broad grass track to another metal gate. Roughly three yards beyond the first gate there is a wooden stile and a yellow waymark arrow. Do not cross over the stile or follow the arrow along this track. Back on the right track, cross over the second gate and continue along the grass track as it runs between the two black/corrugated iron–roofed wooden barns to a third metal gate. Cross over this gate and follow the grass track straight on to a fourth metal gate. At the fourth gate (not painted as often as the Forth Bridge) there is a wooden stile. Cross over stile, following a yellow waymark arrow straight on up the hill along a vehicle-rutted grass track; there are two vehicle-rutted grass tracks that run parallel up the hill, take the one to the left-hand side. Follow the grass track up and down the hill for about 300 yards to a small beck and a yellow-topped waymarker post. On the post there is a yellow waymark arrow, follow this arrow left and continue along the grass track that runs alongside the beck/ditch; keeping the beck/ditch to the immediate left-hand side. Follow this track all the way to Eversden Wood.

② At the yellow-topped waymarker post there is a junction. Continue straight on, following a yellow waymark arrow, and bear immediately right to follow the grass track up a small slope that runs alongside the edge of Eversden Wood. Continue to follow this track, eventually through a gap in a hedgerow, keeping the woodland to the immediate left-hand side.

③ At the corner of the field there is a crossroads. Do not turn left or right here, but instead continue straight ahead along the grass/dirt track, into Eversden Wood. The track eventually leads to a T-junction with a grass track. Turn left at this junction and continue on through the trees. The grass track eventually bears off to the left, at which point there is a gap in the trees (and a blue plastic bin). Pass through this gap to emerge from the woods at a broad, vehicle-rutted grass/dirt track. Turn left at this point and follow the track to a corner of Eversden Wood. At the corner, turn left and follow the grass track alongside the edge of the woodland to a yellow-topped waymarker post. At the post, follow a yellow waymark arrow to bear right, away from woods, and continue on for about 20 yards to a gap in a hedgerow. Pass through the gap and continue on diagonally across a field along a poorly defined but dead straight dirt track; the track may be marked by nothing more than a single pair of shallow vehicle-ruts. The track eventually leads to a waymarker post on the field boundary. At the post, follow a yellow waymark arrow diagonally across the next field, in the same direction as before. Again, the track is poorly defined but dead straight; and again it may be marked by nothing more than a single pair of shallow vehicle-ruts. The track eventually leads down a gentle slope to a vehicle-rutted dirt/grass track. Turn right and follow this track past Merry's Farm to a junction with

Looking east towards Merry's Farm and Great Eversden

a single track, metalled road (Wimpole Road) and a semi-metalled bridleway. Turn left and follow Wimpole Road all the way back to the Hoops.

PLACES OF INTEREST NEARBY

Wimpole Estate, signposted off the A603, 8 miles south-west of Cambridge, consists of a hall, garden and park, and a working farm with many rare breeds. Wimpole Hall is a magnificent country house, and is mainly 18th century in style. Information on opening times and admission charges can be obtained by telephone: 01223 207257.

Horseheath
The Old Red Lion

MAP: OS EXPLORER 210 (GR 609472) | **WALK 28** | **DISTANCE:** 2½ MILES

DIRECTIONS TO START: HORSEHEATH IS SITUATED JUST OFF THE A1307, APPROXIMATELY 4 MILES TO THE WEST OF HAVERHILL. THE OLD RED LION IS LOCATED AT THE FAR WESTERN END OF THE VILLAGE. **PARKING:** IN THE PUB CAR PARK.

This bracing walk passes through an area of attractive countryside surrounded by rolling farmland. Part of the circuit follows the ancient Roman road that originally ran from Cambridge to a settlement near present day Horseheath. The village itself is situated close to the Suffolk border, and is home to the Gothic-styled 15th-century church of All Saints. In the church there is a 14th-century brass of a knight in full armour; sadly though, the inscription to the brass is lost. Outside, on the boundary wall near the entrance to the church, there is a plaque commemorating a visit to the church made by King George V in 1912. The plaque reads:

George V RI our King, in mellow
autumn tide
Here viewed a blooodless fray;
May duty, love and peace abide
To bless him day by day.

Army Manoeuvres, Sep 18, 1912.

The Old Red Lion

This 18th-century inn is partly stone-flagged and heavily timbered, and has lots of nooks and crannies to explore, including a restaurant adorned with brasses and beams. The Old Red Lion is open on Monday to Saturday from 12 noon to 11 pm and on Sunday from 12 noon to 10.30 pm, and food is served every day from 12 noon to 2 pm and 7 pm to 9 pm.

The beers are Marston's Pedigree, John Smith's Bitter, Theakston's XB and guest ales. You will also find a selection of bottled ales and an extensive range of wines. Bar snacks are on offer or you can choose from sumptuous menus in the friendly and relaxed atmosphere of the restaurant; it's not a bad combination. Accommodation is available here too. Telephone: 01233 892909.

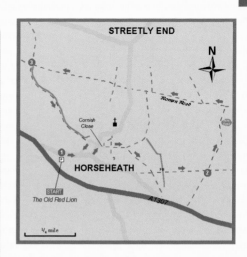

The Walk

① From the Old Red Lion turn right and follow the main road into Horseheath. At the triangular road junction turn left, following the sign to West Wickham for about 100 yards. Turn right onto Cornish Close, and continue on for another 50 yards, after which there is a grass track that runs between houses to the left, from which it is fenced off, and a hedgerow by the roadside. Follow the grass track straight on for about 50 yards, after which there is a wooden stile. Cross over the stile, following the yellow waymark arrow, and continue on along the grass track (do not follow either of the tracks to the left or to the right at this junction). After about 100 yards there is a gap in the hedgerow; pass through this gap and follow the straight dirt track directly across the field towards a white-walled barn (again, do not follow either of the tracks to the left or to the right at this junction). Eventually the dirt track leads to a junction between two tracks. Turn left at this junction and follow the track over a small wooden footbridge and up the hill; the track follows alongside power lines eventually to a gap in a hedgerow.

② Turn left at the gap in the hedgerow (at the top of the hill) and follow the grass track, keeping the hedgerow to the right-hand side. There is a better pathway to the left-hand side of the hedgerow, but, strictly speaking, this is not a public right of way. At the end of the hedgerow continue following the track straight on, towards the woods, this time keeping the fence line to the right-hand side. The track eventually leads past Acre Pond to a metal gate at the corner of the field. After the metal gate, turn left and follow the gravel track down the hill in the general direction of Horseheath. The gravel track eventually leads to a main road; cross over, and on the other side of the road follow the public

The route along the ancient Roman road

bridleway sign straight on (do not pass through the metal gate at this point, as there is no public right of way beyond it). The bridleway runs tightly between two hedgerows for approximately 400 yards, before opening out at a crossroads with a public footpath. Continue straight on at this junction, keeping the hedgerow to the right-hand side.

③ Turn left at the bottom of the hill. Follow the track, which passes through the dip between the hills, back to Horseheath. A small beck runs along the left-hand side of this track all the way back to the village. At the end of the track, just before the houses, there is a stile. Cross over the stile

and follow the track between the houses to a metalled footpath. Bear right and follow the metalled footpath between the houses to the main road. Turn right and follow the main road back to the Old Red Lion.

PLACES OF INTEREST NEARBY

Linton Zoo, just off the A1307 west of Horseheath, is about 10 miles south-east of Cambridge, on the south-western outskirts of Linton. Wildlife and gardens are set in 10 acres of countryside. It is open from 10 am to dusk, with last admission 45 minutes before closing. Telephone: 01223 891308 or 0891 424201 (for 24 hour recorded information). Lots of big cats.

Hinxton
The Red Lion

MAP: OS EXPLORER 209 (GR 496450) WALK 29 DISTANCE: 3 MILES

DIRECTIONS TO START: EXIT THE M11 AT JUNCTION 10, THEN FOLLOW THE A505 EAST TO A ROUNDABOUT WITH THE A1301. FROM THE ROUNDABOUT FOLLOW THE A1301 SOUTH FOR ABOUT 1 MILE TO THE TURN OFF FOR HINXTON. **PARKING:** IN THE PUB CAR PARK.

The walk mainly follows green lanes and field boundaries, but there is also a bit of the River Cam and a few trees to be savoured. Hinxton itself is a quiet village, lying in the valley of the River Cam. The Grade II listed Hinxton Hall is situated about 150 yards south of the Red Lion. Nowadays it is home to three scientific institutes which together form one of the highest concentrations of expertise in the field of biological research.

The Red Lion

The highly popular Red Lion is a sympathetically extended 16th-century coaching inn, brimming with character and atmosphere from its wood-beamed ceilings to its varnished wooden floorboards. There are many snugs and an abundance of pictures, brasses, clocks and other bric-a-brac. Outside there is also a terraced beer garden and a wooden dove tower.

Opening times on Monday to Saturday are from 11 am to 2.30pm and 6 pm to 11 pm; on Sunday from 12 noon to 2.30 pm and 7 pm to 10.30 pm. The beers include Adnams Bitter, Greene King IPA and Woodforde's Wherry, as well as a selection of bottled ales. Food is available every day from 12 noon to 2 pm and from 7 pm to 9.30 pm. There is a separate dining area, but bar food is served too. Telephone: 01799 530601.

The Walk

① From the pub turn right and follow the main road (High Street) to Mill Lane. Turn left at Mill Lane and continue on to the junction with Duxford Road. Turn left at this junction and follow Duxford Road, eventually across a footbridge over a ford and then a railway level-crossing. Roughly 150 yards beyond the level-crossing there is a public footpath sign and a wooden stile. Turn left here and follow the sign over the stile and along a broad dirt track. Where the track passes next to the end of a straight hedgerow, turn right and follow a narrow dirt track along the edge of that hedgerow, keeping the hedgerow to the immediate left-hand side.

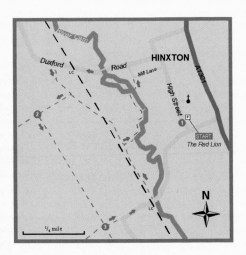

② Turn left at the waymarker post and follow the yellow waymark arrow through a gap in the hedgerow and then roughly south-east along a straight, broad dirt track. After ¼ mile or so the track comes to a field boundary junction (and a 90° angle in the direction of the overhead three-way power lines). Continue straight on at this point, in the same direction as before, along a broad (and in the winter months, muddy) bridleway. The three-way power lines also follow the route of the bridleway, which leads to a gap between two hedgerows which mark the boundaries of two fields. Continue straight on along the bridleway as it runs between the two hedgerows and then on into a small wood.

③ Turn left at the junction and continue on along a vehicle-rutted dirt track to a main road. Turn left and follow the road in the direction of Hinxton. Just beyond the railway level-crossing, turn left and follow the public footpath sign along a grass track which runs between two hedgerows and parallel with the railway line. Follow the track for about ¼ mile to a metal/wooden

The ford across Duxford Road

kissing-gate. Pass through the kissing-gate and follow the yellow waymark arrow along the grass/dirt track to the right; ie do not bear left and continue along the track that runs between the thick hedgerows, parallel with the railway lines. Follow the grass/dirt track as it snakes along the edge of the field and, for much of the way, the riverside (River Cam). At the junction with the permissive way, roughly ¼ mile along the track, bear left and continue on to a junction by a wooden footbridge. Turn right at the junction and cross over the footbridge. On the other side of the footbridge, continue straight on the 10 yards or so to the junction with another dirt track. Bear left at this junction and follow the track along the riverside, across two sluice gates, to a wooden kissing-gate.

Beyond the sluice gates the track passes housing and runs for part of the way between two wooden fence lines. Go through the kissing-gate, bear right and follow Mill Lane back to the High Street, then turn right and follow the High Street back to the Red Lion.

PLACES OF INTEREST NEARBY
Imperial War Museum, Duxford, off junction 10 of the M11, north-west of Hinxton. There are hundreds of aircraft of all types and vintages on display, in several large hangars and out in the open. Many flying displays and events are also held throughout the summer season. Duxford is open all year round, but closes a couple of hours earlier in the winter months. For further information, including opening times and admission charges, telephone: 01223 835000.

Abington Pigotts
The Pig & Abbot

MAP: OS EXPLORER 208 (GR 306444) | WALK 30 | DISTANCE: 5 MILES

DIRECTIONS TO START: FOLLOW THE A1198 TO KNEESWORTH AND THEN HEAD WEST TOWARDS BASSINGBOURN. PASS STRAIGHT THROUGH BASSINGBOURN AND ON TO LITLINGTON, FROM WHERE YOU FOLLOW THE SIGNS TO ABINGTON PIGOTTS. **PARKING:** IN THE PUB CAR PARK.

The walk mainly follows quiet country lanes, via the villages of Abington Pigotts, Litlington and Steeple Morden (with a pub in each). Abington Pigotts is about 1,000 years old. According to the Domesday Book, in 1086 it had 17 inhabitants, and there are only 100 or so these days. Its small size and largely isolated setting ensure that it remains wonderfully aloof from the outside world.

The Pig & Abbot

After it had been threatened with closure, the Pig & Abbot was bought by a consortium of locals in 1997. The fight to save it made the local and national press, and the newspaper clippings telling the story are on display in the pub. Inside, the building is quite atmospheric. It has wood-beam ceilings, brass plaques and plates, a real fire in winter and a few decorative old agricultural implements scattered about. There is also a pleasant beer garden, just perfect for those hot summer day (sic).

The pub is open on Monday to Thursday from 11 am to 3 pm and from 7 pm to 11 pm; on Friday to Saturday it is open all day from 11 am to 11 pm; on Sunday from 12 noon to 10.30 pm. Adnam's Bitter, City of Cambridge Brewery Boathouse Bitter, Jennings Cocker Hoop and Woodforde's Great Eastern are the beers on offer. Bottled ales and a good wine selection are also available. The well prepared, tasty food is served on Monday to Saturday from 12 noon to 2.30 pm and from 7 pm to 9.30 pm and on Sunday from 12 noon to 9 pm. Telephone: 01763 853515.

The Walk

① From the pub turn right and follow the road for approximately 1⅓ miles to Litlington. At Litlington the road ends at a junction by a church (St Catherine's). If you want to visit the Crown public house, turn left at this junction. Otherwise, take the road to the right of the church and continue for about 100 yards before turning right, opposite The Old Vicarage, and following the public footpath sign to

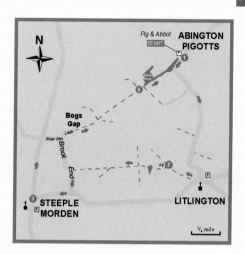

Steeple Morden (1¼ miles).

② Do not cross over the small wooden footbridge. Instead, turn left and follow the track along the line of the hedgerow, keeping the hedgerow to the right-hand side. At the end of the hedgerow continue on, bearing slightly right, towards a copse of trees. Cross over a semi-metalled track, just before reaching the copse, and continue on in the same direction as before, eventually reaching a gap in the trees. At the gap continue straight on along a dirt track through the copse (roughly 10 yards). On the other side of the copse follow the dirt track straight on across a field, up a gentle slope to a dirt track crossroads; do not follow the path to the left upon emerging from the copse. Continue straight ahead at the crossroads, following the broad, vehicle-rutted dirt/grass track west for about ⅔ mile to a metalled road (Brook End). Turn left and follow Brook End to a junction, then turn right and follow the road to Steeple Morden.

③ To visit the Wagon & Horses public

The path to Brook End

house, turn left here. Otherwise, turn right and follow the road north, past several colourful houses, and, if its summertime, perhaps even a game of village cricket on the recreation ground. After about ²/₃ mile there is a crossroads. Turn right here and follow Bogs Gap Lane to a junction with Brook End. At the junction, turn left and continue to follow Bogs Gap Lane (a dead-end road) to the end of the metalled road surface at Bogs Gap. Follow the public bridleway sign at Bogs Gap and continue straight on along the bridleway towards Bibles Grove.

④ Continue straight on at the junction, following the blue waymark arrow to another junction at the corner of Bibles Grove. Continue straight on at this junction, following a yellow waymark arrow and keeping Bibles Grove to the left-hand

side. The track eventually leads to a gate by some cottages. Pass through the gate and follow the gravel driveway straight on to reach a metalled road. Turn left and follow the metalled road back to the Pig & Abbot.

PLACES OF INTEREST NEARBY

The Shuttleworth Collection is in Old Warden village, about 9½ miles west of Abington Pigotts. This is a unique collection of historic aircraft and vehicles, all kept in working order. Follow the A1 to the Biggleswade north roundabout, then exit onto the B658, following the signs to Old Warden. On entering Old Warden there is a sharp right-hand bend. The entrance to The Shuttleworth Collection is on the left at this bend. The Collection is open all year round, and there are flying displays in the summer months. Further information on opening times and entrance prices can be obtained by telephone: 01767 626200.